CONCILIUM

Religion in the Eighties

CONCILIUM

Concilium 131 (1/1980): Sociology of Religion

WORK AND RELIGION

Edited by
Gregory Baum

English Language Editor
Marcus Lefébure

T. & T. CLARK
Edinburgh

THE SEABURY PRESS
New York

1980

T. & T. Clark Ltd., 36 George Street, Edinburgh EH2 2LQ

ISBN: 0 567 30011 0

The Seabury Press, 815 Second Avenue, New York, N.Y. 10017

ISBN: 0 8164 2273 7

Library of Congress Catalog Card No.: 80 50 422

Printed in Scotland by William Blackwood & Sons Ltd., Edinburgh

Concilium: Monthly except July and August.

Subscriptions 1980: All countries (except U.S.A. and Canada) £23·00 postage and handling included; U.S.A. and Canada $54.00 postage and handling included. (Second class postage licence pending at New York, N.Y.) Subscription distribution in U.S. by Expediters of the Printed Word Ltd., 527 Madison Avenue, Suite 1217, New York, N.Y. 10022.

CONTENTS

Editorial

IN CONTEMPORARY social science much attention is being given to work. To understand the social implications of work it is necessary to study the conditions of work and their impact on human consciousness, the condition of life to which men and women are entitled by their work, and finally the attitude of people toward their own labour. Social scientists become increasingly aware that the work people do has an enormous influence on how they see themselves, how they experience reality, and how they define their own humanity. Work is therefore inevitably related to religion. This is true through the last factor mentioned above, the attitude toward work, an aspect especially explored by Max Weber and by a multitude of social researchers after him. What is the economic ethic (*Wirtschaftsethik*) of the world religions and the various branches of Christianity? But since the conditions under which people work in some way affect their consciousness—this aspect was first explored by Karl Marx—work is related to religion also from this point of view. Does industrial labour estrange workers from the spiritual dimension? Does dedication to work in factory and office produce a pragmatic outlook that leads to the waning of religion? These are classical questions in sociology. But since work is connected with a certain standard of life and determines the share men and women have in society's wealth, they may come to oppose traditional religion if they perceive it as the legitimation of the order that exploits them or become its supporter if it upholds the order that allows them to thrive. At the same time it has been argued that in some circumstances people deprived of the goods of life turn to religion as a source of consolation.

Christian theologians have been influenced by sociological considerations and begun to study the relation of work and consciousness. A recent declaration by the French bishops on Euro-Communism (1977) acknowledges the impact of Marxist insights on Christian theology, in particular the recognition that human consciousness is related to the work people do and hence is rooted in the material conditions of life. The Church is learning, therefore, never to preach social justice and human liberation unless this be accompanied by the demand for structural changes affecting the condition of labour and the share in the wealth produced. In some countries the Church is confronted with a pastoral question, the answer to which is by no means easy. Should the Church in face of a society with chronic unemployment demand full employment and continue to promote a piety that leads to dedication and diligence, or should the Church recognise that there is no return to full employment and hence produce a spiritual outlook that enables people to remain humanly and psychically well even if they do not work? Has the time come when the Church must transcend the work ethic?

This volume deals with significant elements that lead to a better understanding of the relation between work and religion. These elements do not build up to a single conclusion. More research and more exploration are required before a consistent theory can emerge.

The first section offers a systematic analysis of the relation between work and religion and presents the positions of the two classical authors, Marx and Weber. The second section presents analyses of concrete situations. Studies of this kind are so important because they usually show that the historical reality does not follow the theoretical anticipations but contains surprises which in turn demand new analysis. The final section looks upon work and religion from a theological point of view.

GREGORY BAUM

PART I

Systematic Presentations

Jean Rémy

Work and Self-awareness

THIS ANALYSIS takes work as its starting-point, singling out for particular attention the conditions of work, the attitude of society concerning economic life and, finally, the living conditions which work imposes on the workers.

These elements constitute a basis which sensitises the various types of workers to certain religious forms and dimensions.

1. CONDITIONS OF WORK

Work, as a material process, is subject to a complex of constraints and possibilities which bears on the problems which have to be, or have been resolved. Thus the farmer, subjected to the hazards of climatic conditions, may be contrasted with those who are involved in trades which are pursued with a regularity which is independent of such constraints. Moreover, the end product of such work is very different in the two cases: making life grow by submitting to the laws of nature, or fashioning a world of objects in the service of some human activity. In the second case one may exalt the quality of human work involved, and attribute value to tasks of conception and realisation. Conception may itself be distinguished from and contrasted with realisation, or the act of fashioning; intellectual work may be opposed to manual work. This social and technical division of labour will permit the establishment of a hierarchy which the world-vision of the community helps to impose on it. This vision does not necessarily ascribe centrality of meaning to the act of making. Thus in sixth-century Greek society, analysed by J. P. Vernant,[1] the art of speaking, of the *logos*, takes priority over that of making things. The speeches which enable one to carry conviction with other men in political assemblies, or intellectual dominance through the sciences, are presented as far superior to manufacturing techniques which belong to the artisan.

This hierarchy is in harmony with the structure of collective life in which politics, or public activity in common, is at the centre of the citizen's life, just as the *agora* is at the centre of the city, as a place of speech-making in which each must convince the others so as to enable democratic control to be exercised over the major political options. The citizen enjoyed the free time in which to do this, since economic life was left to the 'non-citizens'.

There was no question whatsoever of exalting the rôle of the producer in the modern sense of the term, by associating production with the ability to transform the material world. This is all the more evident in that in Greek society the use to which objects were to be put was of decisive importance in their production: the user held the key to their significance, to which the artisan who made them had to conform. The primacy of use-value should not, then, be confused with the primacy of the producer in the control of his product.

On the contrary, economic activities were kept separate from those activities which were described as 'noble'. Primacy was ascribed to intellectual work over manual, to the word over the action. Had this hierarchy not exerted an influence, by way of Greek culture, on Christian thought? . . . And one might wonder about the importance given in the Church of today to the liturgy of the word.

With regard to this exaltation of the word one may ask oneself why popular religion gives priority to actions, so that making a pilgramage on foot, or burning a candle, has more significance than devoting oneself to a commentary on the Scriptures. Used to working with their hands, the working classes, beyond their manual abilities, maintain a close involvement with action, and appreciate its capability of transforming and giving immediate expression to the real. Thus they will ascribe value to an object which they feel instinctively has taken a good deal of time and painstaking workmanship to make ('that's really well made'; 'now that's what you call craftsmanship') and will be less enthusiastic about an object which has an attractive shape but which has not needed much work to produce. They display the same attitude towards the word, which unlike the deed seems to them to be a weak means of tranforming reality and to offer a very limited guarantee of authenticity. Is this not the reason for the scepticism of members of this class about fine speeches of which they can appreciate the eloquence ('he was a good speaker') but in whose efficacity they do not believe? They cannot take such speakers 'at their word' until this word has been tested out by a great many repeated concrete actions.

Such a class displays as great a reluctance concerning the techniques of psychological therapy centred on verbalisation as it does concerning the liturgy which accords a privileged status to verbal expression to the detriment of ritual acts. By contrast, those in the superior position readily attribute to speech a capacity for dominating practical action.

So we see that in the Church of today the importance given to the liturgy of the word in not neutral. It hinders the possibilities of participation and expression enjoyed by various social groups.

2. THE ATTITUDE OF SOCIETY TOWARDS ECONOMIC LIFE

The reversal of attitudes towards the economic sphere in the Christian West can be discerned, particularly, through the evolution of the definition of the poor. In the Middle Ages, the poor man was honoured as the symbol of Jesus Christ, who was to be welcomed with open-handed hospitality. This concept was later replaced by one in which the poor man was considered as a lazy vagabond who had to be locked up in order to be taught the meaning of work and of discipline.[2]

This change of attitude towards the poor was combined with an evolving view of men's relationship with money: the rather dubious legitimacy of a direct involvement with money resulted in the marginal status, and also the power, of the Jew in the history of the Christian West in which a whole complex of symbolism, including the imagery of the cathedrals, associated the Jew with a negative sacredness.[3] But gradually the enhanced status of the economic sphere emerged as a result of the development of the financial system, which, far from being confined to marginal sections of society gradually enabled the new bourgeois to establish itself.

This evolution at the level of social structure would not have been possible without an evolution at the level of the lived experience of meaning, which serves as a frame of reference for a society and establishes the value through which it thinks of itself.[4]

Thus de Certeau[5] was to speak of the 'reversal of the thinkable' between the sixteenth century and later periods. At first the religious was perceived as that which, from the inside, allows the conceptualisation of social conflicts which spontaneously take on the form of theological oppositions. In contrast to this, since the sixteenth century, we have witnessed the emergence of a social morality, which allows the development of a world in which 'natural' rights acquire more significance, and in which public morality gradually ensures the security and the mutual confidence necessary for the extension of the means of exchange. Systems of exchange and the economic life they make possible became central to society. The religious sphere reorganised itself on the basis of this new situation. At the same time, the widening use of instruments encouraged the general use in everyday life of individual calculation: instruments of abstract measurement, independent of subjective perception, such as the clock which allows the multiplication of the calculation of time, and especially of working-time.

As part of a reciprocal process, the development of one's individual value through work became one of the central elements of human dignity. Max Weber has pointed out how much Protestantism, which was in close collaboration with this modern society, contributed to the establishment at the centre of life of the professional or work-ethic. As a result, discipline at work, especially through the apprenticeship of respect for timetables, was one of the objects of working-class education in the last century.

The substitution of regular work for casualness, the sense of a unit of calculation and planning, larger than that of the individual family, education in cleanliness, hygiene, orderliness—were these not so many educational projects, often formulated in terms of moral precepts, which were encouraged in the nineteenth century by enlightened employers, and have been given concrete form since then, thanks to the work of various social agencies which, moreover, originated in them? This type of objective has been taken up in turn by the working-class movement itself in those national contexts into which the new spirit penetrated most deeply, for example the puritan countries of Northern Europe.

This transformation allowed the economic domain to take shape and to become independent from the religious and political spheres. For if the economic dimension is present in all societies, and even has a determining rôle by making available new possibilities in the material realm, it does not necessarily give rise to the formation of an autonomous domain. Thus, as M. Godelier states,[6] economic relationships may take the form, seen from the inside, of kinship ties. Family structures become, in that type of context, the centre in which the social structure is formed, allocating various patterns of solidarity and hierarchy. Even if the family continues to have an important part to play in modern society, its significance is changing.[7] So we find that from one society to another there is a displacement of the area regarded as sacred, if one associates the concept of sacredness with an ambivalent attitude towards a force capable of producing both order and disorder and in relation to which the central concern of a society is felt to be at stake.

Where family and kinship have a decisive rôle, the sacred may take shape initially around sexuality and its regulation. If, on the contrary, the political sphere is central and it is a matter of giving a mystical dimension to the constraints imposed by the law, then at that point the significance of the leader, of obedience, may become the basis from which the sacred originates. If, in a society like our own, the predominance of the economic sphere depends on the imposition of a universal system of rationality, the conflict of the rational and the irrational may be at the heart of the collective exaltation around which deep-rooted loyalties and antagonisms resolve. . . . The association of the sacred with the central concerns of a society allows one to dissociate oneself somewhat from all those theories which link the sacred with a weak control over the forces of nature. Nevertheless, in so doing we are anxious to preserve the distinction between the sacred and the religious: each axis of expression of the sacred is compatible with expressions which may or may not be religious.

3. WORK AND LIVING CONDITIONS

In a society in which the economic sphere is dominant, working relationships may determine living conditions which are very different, which exert and influence on people's aspirations. One may thus contrast groups which live in perpetual insecurity, without any control over their future, with groups which, enjoying a certain degree of security in their existence, are nevertheless afraid of falling back into a condition of poverty, and with groups which live in the certainty of being able to control their future.

Thus certain social groups live their collective life as if it were a game of chance. The game of chance is one in which the players do not know the rules—even if any exist—so that the possibility of putting rational tactics into practice is excluded. The players therefore see the result of their actions as linked to luck. When, as for example among the members of the sub-proletariat, life proceeds like a game of chance—which explains its character, which is both tragic and casual at the same time—everything appears to be attributable to good or bad luck: having a job today and not tomorrow, 'drawing a losing or winning number' in the marriage lottery, having or not having children, living in the last house in the street to be compulsorily purchased, or the first one not to be. . . . This kind of view of oneself and of the situations one lives through does not itself come about by chance: it is rooted in objective conditions of economic insecurity, which are thus transposed onto the plane of subjective hopes and reveal themselves in particular by a sense of the impossibility of making any rational calculation for the future, in whatever area it may be: one is incapable of controlling the expenditure of a large sum of money which suddenly comes one's way, or of planning its use over a more or less long period of time; one feels no concern over birth control or about taking some form of other hygienic precaution, etc. . . .

Explicit mental concepts will thus lead these social classes to imagine the existence of an opposition between the familiar world in which nothing can be controlled and an unfamiliar world which is all-powerful, intervening in the familiar world to apportion benefits or misfortunes, and whose good graces must be conciliated by means of symbolic appropriation rituals, that is to say by practices whose efficacity does not derive from one's work.

The logic of exclusion which is associated with this typical sub-proletarian ethos can only be understood with reference to the economic rules which govern an advanced capitalist society, based on the stimulation of individualised calculation. In effect, the marginal status of such an ethos is not revealed in the same way in a traditional society, in which there is also a lack of individual control over time and the future. In such a society, this lack is integrated into a coherent understanding of a cosmic order, in which one does not make plans for the future, since the future belongs to God; 'The birds do not spin, and our heavenly Father provides for them. . .'

In contrast to the game of chance, the game which has rules assumes that the player has a perfect knowledge of the rules which govern it and, because of this knowledge, a tactical capability directed towards the improvement or the reversal of his position.

This view is one which distinguishes the working-class milieu of the proletariat. The more regular nature of their work, their corporate association within the context of a collective mechanism of which they are not the owners but whose activity they are capable of preventing by collective strike action, gives them a feeling of power. Thus workers' movements develop in a way that leads to the perfecting of collective practices in working life and, especially through the introduction of collective bargaining, encourages the idea that the two sides of industry have conflicting interests.

If collective action has a privileged place amongst the working classes, individual action is seen to be favoured amongst the middle classes, which feel strongly that ethical value should be attributed to individual effort. The result is that there is an opposition between these two ethical systems which explains, for example, why representatives of the middle classes are scandalised at the sight of workers enjoying increased income and various benefits without having 'deserved' to possess such advantages through systematic effort and an increased commitment to their work. By contrast, the working-class ethic tends to consider that collective problems cannot be resolved be demanding individual effort and sacrifice from the workers and that only a modification of the collective context can improve the situation of each individual. Thus there may exist a different attitude within the two groups towards established rules, with one group accepting them on a short-term basis with the prospect of changing them in the longer term, and the other considering that the stability of these rules is the very condition of its own advancement.

A morality of authenticity is clearly in harmony with the situation of the middle class. In their case, social rules only have meaning in so far as they form the basis of the ethical rules. On the other hand, other social groups are more ready to allow a 'double language'. Thus, a working-class group will accept more easily a double language in its relationships with other social groups whose co-operation it must in some way ensure without itself becoming alienated by adopting their criteria of evaluation. In the same way, in their dealings with employers or the clergy working-class groups will accept the need to behave in the way they imagine that the masters of the social game require. It seems to them to be an honest practice in so far as it allows them to enjoy advantages which these masters are alone able to bestow. The double language is not only associated with this particular kind of relationship. It may also be practised by someone in a strong social position whose multiplicity of involvements with other groups allows him, on the one hand, to perceive more clearly the relativity of rules and, on the other hand, gives added value to the ability to adapt one's languages to one's various audiences so as not to provoke the opposite reaction to the one anticipated.

In the game which has rules it is also possible to vary one's tactics according to whether one is playing for maximum gains or minimum risks. To be able to play one's social life for maximum gains one must have absorbed into oneself objective forms of security. This, because of the security he enjoys in the economic and relational spheres, allows someone from a superior class to ascribe high value to gratuitousness, to accept hazardous decisions in the sure knowledge that he will not fall into poverty or suffer social exclusion. Thus someone in a superior social position may be characterised by a certain ease of manner in society, in which he tends to affirm his quality of being in terms of disinterestedness.

Someone from a working-class milieu, on the other hand, may organise his view of himself around a reflex concerned with a secure social position, in which he seeks to multiply means of protection against the hazards of life and the insecurity which might well come back one day. . . . Faced with some project for the future, such a person will readily play to minimise the risk. This explains, for example, the difference which is evident in the recruitment patterns of the various university departments: young people from the more favoured social groups are more ready to enter new subject-areas, with uncertain job prospects, whereas young people from working-class backgrounds opt more often for well-established departments, leading on to secure and stable career patterns.[8]

This system of security and risk is nevertheless subject to change. So, for example, if certain traditionally stable economic sectors find themselves, at a given moment, threatened with insecurity, there is every likelihood that that section of the bourgeois who are involved will change from a risk-taking pattern of behaviour to a defensive one and will therefore change their strategy: instead of the openness and the readiness to take risks which characterised them previously, they will become preoccupied with rigidity and protectionism. Thus there are questions to be asked about the different attitudes which certain sections of the bourgeois might adopt towards changes within the Church. Integrism, for example, is not randomly distributed with respect to these defensive reflexes.

4. REAL LIFE AND IMAGINARY WORLDS

Social life necessarily involves the intervention of imaginary worlds, that is to say not governed by the rules which are enforced in everyday life in the present. These worlds are products of our ability to imagine things differently. These mental pictures allow both the establishment of a certain distance between oneself and the immediate data of daily life and also their transfiguration. This imaginative capacity, like the collective representations which result from it, should in no way be interpreted as if they were necessarily false imaginings or escapist worlds. Nevertheless, the different social classes maintain different modes of relationship with these imaginary worlds. These classes are important determining influences on their possible consciousness.

These imaginary sequences, unfettered by the rules of everyday life, allow elements to be structured in a similar way to the oneiric world, the world of dreams. To refer these imaginary worlds to the oneiric registers is particularly important for the sub-proletarian class which, lacking any ability to exert control at the level of real life, finds that this other world opens the way to all kinds of possibilities. What is more, this class intermingles the two registers to the point at which it can no longer distinguish them clearly from each other. This is all the more true in that, since life is lived as if it were a game of chance, relationships with imaginary worlds are lived out as relationships with so many forces which must be conciliated and from which marvellous results are expected.

It is the opposite reflex which dominates the consciousness of the working class, which seeks to extend as far as possible the limits of the register of real life and rejects the involvement of the latter with the code of the dream, which it associates with weakness. Such an attitude forms the basis of the working-class world which—even including the aesthetic domain in which a painting has to represent something—values facts and mistrusts fine words and for which the whole structure of social life is governed by the principle of identity, according to which A = A. In many ways this attitude contributes to the strength of this social group, but it is also in danger of constituting its weakness: thus, for example, if it leads this class to multiply those actions of daily life which reinforce the affirmation of its total solidarity with all those who share the same kinds of insecurity, it also leads it to express its dissensions through acts of physical violence, and to refuse to allow these conflicts to be expressed more indirectly by multiplying social rituals.

Other social groups will take pleasure in being able to draw on imaginary worlds and the registers of real life at the same time, without, however, confusing them. Thus certain groups will enjoy seeing plays in which they are treated ironically, without feeling uneasy and wishing to alter straight away their reactions in everyday life. Since they are capable of a certain degree of detachment, they can be helped by these imaginary worlds to confront the future, or else these worlds may provide them with substitute realms which help them to pass beyond certain tensions of their daily lives.

We see, then, that the existence of a variety of possible types of consciousness leads to the fact that, in certain groups, the oneiric register is not distinguished from real life and leads to a close moral identification with the characters represented; for others, it allows the present to be dismantled, to permit the emergence of a forward-looking imagination and to allow a future to be glimpsed which may be very different from the present.

These few observations seem to us to be important for the understanding of the different relationships which the various social groups have with the religious domain, as much as with the literary or artistic domains.

In this analysis, the religious sphere has been set in a global social dynamic as an indispensable element which contributes as much to its stability as to its transformation. With this as one's starting-point one may understand both the similarity of aspirations, as far as the religious sphere is concerned, which one finds between one society and another, as well as the differences which may mark the close involvement of the religious element in different societies and in different social groups. From this point of view work is a sensitive area in so far as it is a determining element of the conditions of existence even if it is not always at the core of the meaning which a society claims to value.

Translated by L. H. Ginn

Notes

1. J. P. Vernant *Mythe et pensée chez les Grecs* (Paris 1963), especially 1, ch. 3 'L'Organisation de l'espace'.
2. P. Grell *L'Organisation de l'assistance publique* (Brussels 1976).
3. F. Raphael 'Le Juif et le diable dans la civilisation de l'occident' in *Social Compass* (1972) XV, 4 pp. 549-567.
4. J. Rémy, L. Voye, E. Servais *Produire ou reproduire? Une sociologie de la vie quotidienne* (Brussels 1978) I, p. 228. A good number of the questions which are treated in this article form part of a wider series of problems to which this work provides an introduction.
5. M. de Certeau 'L'inversion du pensable—L'Histoire religieuse du XVIIe siècle' p. 130; 'Du système religieux à l'éthique des lumières XVII–XVIII' pp. 182–210 in *L'Ecriture de l'histoire* (Paris 1975).
6. M. Godelier *Rationalité et irrationalité de l'économie* (Paris 1969) pp. 291–292.
7. J. Rémy 'The Family: Contemporary Models and Historical Perspective' *Concilium* 121 (1/1979) 3–14.
8. P. Bourdieu *Les Héritiers* (Paris 1968).

Otto Maduro

Labour and Religion according to Karl Marx

1. LABOUR ACCORDING TO MARX

ONE OF the most striking things in the writings of Marx is the emphasis he lays on human labour. We could say, in effect, that Marx's theory of society starts from the hypothesis that the concrete conditions in which human labour is performed are the foundation and the heart of all other human activity. In consequence, if we wish to know, understand and explain some other aspect of human activity, we should first give some other aspect of human activity, we should first give serious attention to the specific conditions in which human labour is performed at the time and place in which we are studying that other aspect of human activity; and starting from such a study of the context we should try to elucidate how those conditions limit and influence that other aspect. Labour, then, is established by Marx as the *ratio essendi* and *ratio cognoscendi* of the whole of human society and of any of its aspects.

What is the reason for this hypothesis that the concrete conditions in which human labour is performed are the foundation and the heart of all other human activity? Marx believes that, to be able to engage in any other activity, human beings need to live; but, to be able to live, those same human beings need to produce material resources sufficient for their survival . . . and they also need to reproduce biologically. So, to produce and reproduce material resources sufficient to meet their need to survive, human beings have to work—that is to say, they have to transform the natural world around them. And such a process of transformation needs to be constant, collective and organised. Therefore, to be able to live, human beings need to reproduce constantly the same human *collectivity* to which they belong (i.e., to reproduce biologically), to reproduce, similarly, the *means of production* (tools, roads, etc.), and to reproduce, finally, the *social relationships* in which they have organised themselves for the purpose of producing resources with a view to their survival. If any of these material conditions of human labour ceases for a longer or shorter time, the community dies and all other human activity in that place ceases as well.

If follows then that the possibility of any other human activity (including religion) must always be conditional upon productive, material human labour. And it follows equally that any other human activity is conditioned by the organisation of labour, since, if another activity—whatever it may be—threatens the reproduction of the concrete conditions of labour in a given society, the spontaneous reaction will be to safeguard those conditions at the expense of that other activity.

2. THE SOCIAL ORGANISATION OF LABOUR

For Marx, the *relations of production* of a community—that is to say, the way in which a community organises itself in order to produce and reproduce the material means necessary for its survival—do not depend solely or mainly upon the will of its members. The relations of production by which a community organises its labour depend, before all and above all, upon its material *productive strength*—that is to say, upon the limited resources on which such a community can count in order to work (the number of its members, available natural resources, implements of work known and accessible, etc.). The extent to which particular material resources are accessible will make the social organisation of labour possible in some forms and impossible in others. Thus, on the basis of the limits of its material resources and by means of particular relations of production, each society organises its survival through a specific *mode of production.*

So, then, human labour is never abstract labour, but labour organised in a concrete mode of production characterised by certain relations between the groups involved in the different aspects of production. And, in so far as this concretely organised labour is what alone makes possible and guarantees human survival (and any activity at all on the part of the human beings involved in it, including religion), to that extent the *reproduction* of the mode of production—and of the relations of production which characterise it—becomes a vital requirement of human existence. In this way, every human activity other than production remains conditional upon, limited by and directed by the need to reproduce the relations of production of that particular community.

3. LABOUR AND HUMAN SPIRITUAL PRODUCTION

Human beings do not produce only their material means of life. The activity of human beings cannot be reduced to material labour, to economics. That is certain. And Marx—in spite of his successors and his enemies—never tried to reduce the human person to a *Homo oeconomicus*. What happens is that Marx, in opposition to the 'idealism' characteristic of the German philosophers of his generation, underlines the importance of the material conditions governing the social organisation of labour for the origin and development of all the other activities which take place in a society. And similarly he emphasises the helpfulness of *knowing* the economic context for understanding the origin, the structure and the social functions of those other activities.

Among those other activities (whose origin, structure and functions are so deeply marked by the social organisation of labour in the society in which they take place) is to be found human spiritual production. Philosophy, theology, science, political theory, law and ethics are, all of them, forms of human spiritual production. Marx never made the mistake of denying the reality, the necessity, the value, the importance, the influence and the relative autonomy of human spiritual production. No. What happens is that Marx rejects every conception which regards human spiritual production as the result of pure intuition, of direct revelation, of mere will, of unconditioned reason or of simple spontaneity. And equally he is against every conception which regards ideas as *the* decisive factor governing the future course of history. That is to say, Marx believes that human spiritual production is neither independent of nor uninfluenced by the social organisation of labour. On the contrary, Marx thinks that all human spiritual production, every *theory*, is mediated and conditioned—in a complex way, but inevitably—by the social organisation of labour in the community where such spiritual production occurs; that is to say, that every theory is closely bound up with a *praxis*.

According to Marx, indeed, human spiritual production (theory) finds in the social organisation of labour (in the praxis) the permanent and indispensable material condition of its existence. And not only that: the praxis limits and directs spiritual production. That is to say, whether or not the production of a theory is possible, along what lines it will develop, how it is to be propagated and interpreted, what role it may play and what influence it may have on history—all these are questions that cannot be decided by the individual (or institution) producing the theory. It is the social organisation of labour in the community in which a theory is produced which will determine the limits and directions of its origin, its structure, its development and its social functions.

We do not see the world as we would like to see it. We see it in such a form and in such a manner as we are permitted to by the praxis in which we are established, by the social position in which the social organisation of labour in our community has placed us. This is, as I see it, one of the central theses of Marx. In consequence, since all theoretical production (including religion) is mediated by a praxis, it is necessary to analyse the social organisation of labour in the place where a theory is produced in order to gain a *concrete* understanding of the theory—that is to say, an understanding of it in the context of the social totality. In other words, the analysis of the social conditions under which a theory is produced is an indispensable requisite for a concrete understanding of the theory.

4. ALIENATED LABOUR AND SPIRITUAL PRODUCTION

One particular type of society, for obvious reasons, attracts the attention of Marx: those societies which are divided into *classes*. Analysing them, Marx finds that they are characterised by the fact that in them the principal means of production are the *private property* of a minority. This makes it possible for the minority to have power to decide on the production, the exchange, the distribution and the consumption of the goods necessary for the survival of the community. Such power makes this minority into a *ruling class*, enjoying privileges which can only be maintained by the reproduction of the relations of production in which the minority is dominant. In such societies, the social organisation of labour is achieved through *relations of domination*, relations of exploitation, which revolve around the private appropriation by that minority of the principal means of production.

Labour, in societies where the class-structure exists, is characterised by Marx as *alienated labour*. Labour is alienated in those societies because the worker, the direct producer of material goods, is not master of his means of production, nor of the conditions under which he works, nor of the final result of his efforts. His labour puts him in a distinct social class—that of the workers. The worker sees himself as a stranger in relation to his work, in relation to what he produces, in relation to himself, and in relation to his divided community. The *social division of labour* introduced by private property converts the worker not into a subject, but into an object, into a mere means of production, lacking the capacity to decide his own fate, or that of his labour, or that of the result of his labour. The workers become, then, a *dominated class*.

The division of labour typical of societies where the class-structure exists—and particularly marked under capitalism—leads to the separation and opposition of *manual labour* and *intellectual labour*, concentrated respectively (at first) in the countryside and the city. These distinct groups, separated spatially and socially, perform on the one hand the work of material production, and on the other that of spiritual production. Spiritual production (philosophical, theological, scientific, political, juridical and moral) is then achieved—progressively more so—in an environment socially and spatially close to the dominant groups. It is sustained by the material production of the manual workers, but enjoys the leisure and privileges denied to them, being so far removed from the environments and living conditions of the workers and peasants. The manual worker has neither the power, nor the time, nor the education, nor the strength to devote himself to such spiritual production as is socially legitimate, and so he sees himself reduced to the condition of consumer of the urban spiritual production. The products of the human spirit become progressively more remote, more alien, more strange. Economic alienation develops into spiritual alienation.

But—moreover—intellectual production, being subject to the interests of those who dominate material production (whose environment and privileges the intellectuals partially share), is turned into an instrument for bringing the consumers of ideas (the manual workers) into submission to the dominant relations of production. The intellectuals, who are spatially and socially close to the dominant classes, and socially and spatially remote from manual labour, tend to produce theories which bear the image and likeness of their own praxis: theories which—quite sincerely—claim to be anterior, exterior and superior to the work of manual production, and which, at the same time, reproduce—in the minds of producers and consumers—the established social order. This is what Marx calls *ideology*: theory which is selfishly ignorant of its link with praxis. And—as he himself affirms—in societies where the class-structure exists, the dominant ideas are the ideas of the ruling class. Ideology—theory which is convinced of its absolute autonomy—is, in general, *dominant ideology*: theory in the service of the perpetuation of alienated labour.

5. THE TRIPLE ALIENATION OF RELIGION UNDER THE REGIME OF PRIVATE PROPERTY

Religion, according to Marx, does not escape the dialectic of alienated labour. Let us now go beyond what Marx actually says, and attempt to develop his analysis of alienated labour as we make a study of religion, leaving aside, for the moment, the problem of Marxian atheism.

In those societies in which the division of labour issues in a separation between manual and intellectual labour, religion, in so far as it represents the work of spiritual production, tends to become alienated labour. The concentration of the religious producers in milieux which are socially and spatially different and distant from those of manual workers—city workers and peasants—leads to a private appropriation and monopolisation of the work of religious production (theology, ethics, liturgy, etc.).

A first aspect of this alienation consists in the fact that religion is not a production of the community. Religious production is concentrated in the hands of specialists (theologians, priests, etc.), who—*de facto* and unconsciously—operate an expropriation of the manual workers' capacity for religious production. In consequence the manual workers find themselves reduced to the condition of passive consumers of a religious production developed outside their interests, their preoccupations and their aspirations. This is *alienation*.

A second aspect of this alienation of religion is to be found in the fact that religious production, developed in close proximity to the dominant milieux and sharing in their privileges and way of life, reproduces—*sub specie aeternitatis*—the dominant interests. Religious institutions tend to be structured in the image and likeness of the social order, and to develop—*de facto* and unconsciously—a spiritual production which will lead to the reproduction of the established order and of the privileges attached to the socially legitimate monopoly of religious production enjoyed by such institutions. The consumption of religious products developed socially and spatially far from the milieux of the workers and peasants becomes an instrument for the sacralisation of alienated labour: *opium of the people*.

A third and final aspect of this alienation of religion consists in the distance—social and spatial—which separates religious production from manual labour. Religious producers, away from the material labour which makes life possible for them and which conditions their own intellectual products, end up believing that their products are completely independent of the social organisation of labour, and spontaneously reject even the suggestion that the development and application of those products is in any way socially conditioned. Similarly, the religious consumers—workers and peasants—away from the process of intellectual production which allows them to think of the world in a religious way and which conditions their own attitude to manual labour, end up thinking that their religion is anterior, exterior and superior to their own labour. Here is the *ideology*.

Alienation, opium of the people and ideology—these three aspects of the alienation of religion under the regime of private property—cross-fertilise and reinforce each other in such a way as to bring about—*de facto*—the reproduction of the same regime of private property which produced the alienation in the first place.

6. ATHEISM AS AN UNSUCCESSFUL ATTEMPT TO LIBERATE RELIGION

The dominated classes are never merely dominated, passively exploited. In every society where the class-structure exists, the expropriation and exploitation of the workers by the owners generates an opposition of interests, a conflict—below the surface or openly declared, according to the circumstances—between workers and owners. In this *class struggle* inherent in every social organisation of alienated labour, those who are dominant make a constant effort to reproduce—at every level, including that of religion—the alienation of labour and their own dominant position. Those who are dominated, for their part, try—at every level, including that of religion—to reappropriate the conditions of production and reproduction of their own life, to revolutionise the social organisation of labour in which they themselves occupy a subordinate position. The outcome of such a class struggle is never determined in advance, nor can it be decided once for all. Such an outcome—which by definition is contingent—depends on the objective and subjective conditions of the classes involved in the struggle, on their respective strength (which is variable), and on circumstantial factors which are often beyond the foresight and control of the classes concerned.

So far as religion is concerned, the dominated classes try to reappropriate the conditions of religious production, to take into their own hands and for their own purposes the production of religion. This tendency to 'expropriate the expropriators' in the religious field can be seen as a facet of the attempt by the dominated classes to reappropriate the material conditions of production and reproduction of their life. It is a specific and concrete attempt to reappropriate the conditions of production and reproduction of their own view of the world, with the object of acquiring the power to develop and propagate a view of the world which is no longer adapted to the interests of the owners but to those of the workers. In this sense, religious disputes, heresies and sectarian movements—above all those which have arisen among the subordinate classes—may often be interpreted as movements for the reappropriation of religious production on the part of the dominated classes. The automatic reaction to this situation of the groups which are religiously dominant, for their part, is an attempt to hinder the reappropriation of religious production by the community: the exclusion of heretics and the correction of their innovations by *ad hoc* sociological mechanisms.

In this way of thinking, atheism can be seen as one more example of the attempt to reappropriate the means of production of man's view of the world: an attempt typical of groups (generally belonging to the intellectual *petite bourgeoisie*) which lack sufficient material and cultural power effectively to oppose the *dominant* religious view with a revolutionary religious view capable of holding together in its embrace a majority of the working classes. Thus atheism turns out to be, often, an attempt at the reappropriation of religion. The attempt fails because it lacks a social foundation capable of carrying it to its ultimate conclusion. The sociological weakness which characterises such an attempt obliges its supporters to accept submissively—*de facto* and unconsciously—the official religious definition (that is, disqualification) of it as *atheistic*. When it thus accepts itself as atheistic (i.e., as religiously illegitimate), the attempt becomes an abortive movement for the liberation of religion, an unsuccessful effort for the reappropriation of religion on the part of the subordinate classes.

7. BEYOND MARX AND SOCIOLOGY

It is true that, for Marx, religion is only explicable as the spiritual product of alienated labour—i.e., as alienation, opium of the people and ideology *par excellence*—and the very possibility of revelation is therefore to Marx unworthy of any consideration. However, these Marxian prejudices should not be allowed to become an obstacle preventing Christians from grasping—with humility and integrity—those things contained in the Marxian sociology of religion which are profoundly important and relevant for our own theory and practice.

Most important of all, the Marxian hypotheses which we have examined could be made the point of departure for self-critical theological and pastoral reflection. In fact the hypotheses suggest that the differing social positions of producers of theology and pastoral leaders, on the one hand, and the recipients of religious production, on the other, are not secondary considerations, much less negligible ones. Rather, Marx's hypotheses show, in a way that deserves our serious and constant attention, that the true *interpretation* and the real social *effects* of any religious activity whatever depend more on the social conditions in which such activity develops than on the faith, culture, or good intentions of those who carry it out. Accordingly, it is possible to believe that, in a society where the class-structure exists, a naïve theology and pastoral practice—not self-critical from the sociological point of view—will result *nolens volens* in the strengthening of the exploitation of labour characteristic of such class-ridden societies: the social conditions of the production of religion are not external to religious production; on the contrary, such conditions *constitute* religious action in its social reality and effectiveness. It follows that pastoral action and theological production which are seriously concerned about their own *real social effects* demand—in a post-Marxian situation—a critical knowledge and a self-critical reflection concerning the historico-social conditions of the production of religion, of the significant impact which those conditions have on religious production, and of the real social effects that a religion conditioned in this way tends to produce in its agents and its recipients. Such sociological self-criticism is, since Marx, the indispensable condition of a pastoral theology which—genuinely—does not wish to be alienation, opium of the people and ideology.

But it would appear that, so long as the *religious relations of production* continue to be determined by a *division of religious labour* which sets up a minority as owners of the religious means of production, so long as the majority are kept in the subordinate position of mere consumers of religious production—that is to say, so long as the social form of religious production remains alienated—religion will inevitably continue to be—*de facto* and unconsciously—alienation, opium of the people and ideology. The reappropriation by the community of the conditions under which religious production is carried on would be—on this view—a necessary (but not in itself sufficient) condition for ending the alienation of human material labour. Simply to change the terms of reference and the *content* of theological production does not of itself (so long as the mode of religious production continues to be governed by the logic of alienated labour) constitute an authentic transformation of theology, however much that content may proclaim and call for a free humanity, however much it may scandalise the oppressors and stimulate the struggles of the oppressed. Liberation theology—if it is really to be what it sets out to be—demands an accompanying liberation of theology: it demands criticism, self-criticism and the revolutionary transformation of the dominant social mode of production of theology.

Translated by G. W. S. Knowles

Julien Freund

Work and Religion according to Max Weber

IF WE are to understand the problem that Weber has posed with regard to the relationship between work and religion, we must first situate it within the context of his work as a whole. This leads us to make two preliminary remarks.

1. Weber has seldom directly compared religion with work—he usually introduces a third term, that of ethics, which has to be understood in two ways. On the one hand, there is morality in the strict sense of the word, according to which work is regarded as a duty. Weber has said of this form of morality that 'there has perhaps never been a more intense form of religious valuation of moral activity than that devised by those skilled in Calvinism'.[1] On the other hand, what he also means by ethics is a certain way of behaving. Recalling the condemnation of wealth by the Catholic Church in the Middle Ages and the way in which certain rich people tried to come to a compromise with this *turpitudo*, he has noted that 'those who were sceptical or indifferent became reconciled with the Church by means of gifts. In any case, it seemed better to be insured against the uncertainty of what might happen after death and—at least according to a fairly loose although extremely widespread view—it was enough to submit externally to the commandments of the Church to be assured of salvation. This is the external aspect of morality, which is quite simply immoral, that those who are concerned attach to their own behaviour.'[2] It is as well to remember at this point that Weber believed that religion inspired an ethical behaviour which in turn influenced the way in which the meaning of work was understood. In other words, ethics were for him a roundabout way along which religion helped us to understand work.

2. Weber applied this method to his analysis of religious sociology as a whole. This is clear, for example, in the suggestive sub-title that he gave to his collected essays on religious sociology: 'The Economic Ethics of World Religions'. He drew attention, for example, to the attitude of various religions towards work. He pointed to the angry hostility of Confucianists to Buddhists, who turned the people away from all useful work.[3] He also analysed the caste system in India in connection with the idea of work. It is, however, important to note that the relationship between religion and work was not his central interest in these essays and that he dealt with this relationship either by alluding to it in passing or by making it the subject of rapid surveys or summaries.

In his *Protestant Ethics and the Spirit of Capitalism*, on the other hand, he was centrally concerned with this question throughout almost the whole book. This is why I shall refer principally to this work in what follows, although the restrictions imposed by the length of this article also play a part in this rather narrow choice. I shall also, however, take into account certain views expressed in Weber's *Wirtschaft und Gesellschaft*.

1. FREE LABOUR

Bearing in mind the nature of the question that we are trying to answer here, we cannot consider the whole of Weber's theory of work and especially the way in which he discussed it in the second chapter of his *Wirtschaft und Gesellschaft*. All that we are able and need to do here is to look at one or two aspects.

In the first place, he made a distinction between 'obligatory trade or profession' and a 'free choice of trade'.[4] He also pointed, in the case of free work, to the fact that there are different possible ways in which man can be attached to his trade. In addition to the attachment based on feeling and traditional attachment, there is also rational attachment. He gave an interesting definition of the latter: 'In its typical form, rational attachment is determined either by religious motives or by a particularly exalted social evaluation of work as such. It has been proved by experience that all the other motives are transitory in nature.'[5] This statement brings us to the very heart of Weber's problem, since it places side by side the concept of rational work and religious motivation.

According to Weber, most civilisations have lived under a rule of servile labour in various forms, some more and some less hard. It is only in the West, under the influence of Christianity (although this has by no means been the only cause), that the social structure of trades and professions has, with the help of the guilds that were created, moved gradually towards a total emancipation of labour and the elimination of all forms of slavery. A very clear understanding of the meaning of trade as a free profession organised institutionally with a complete procedure of apprenticeship was present in the trade guilds.

Weber, however, insisted on another aspect of free labour, which, he believed, had two basic consequences—an economic and a social consequence. The economic consequence came about as the result of capitalism, seen as the rational organisation of free labour and it existed only as a very vague outline in other civilisations.[6] Precise calculation in advance, in other words, economic forecasting, 'is only possible on the basis of free labour'.[7] The social consequence came about with the appearance of the proletariat, which 'as a class, could not exist in the absence of all enterprise in which free labour is organised. The 'class struggle' exists everywhere in various forms—between creditors and debtors, owners of land and landless peasants, serfs or farmers, merchants and consumers and so on. Apart from Europe, however, the struggles between capital and labour that began in the West in the late Middle Ages and led to the sharp antagonism between the great industrial employers and their free, paid workers in modern society are known only in an embryonic form or else not at all. This accounts for the absence of problems that are similar to those known to contemporary socialism.'[8]

Weber's fundamental conviction was that communism may have been known in other societies, but that these societies have only ever had a very vague idea of socialism. His real originality, however, is to have shown that there are very many different sources of modern capitalism—including, for example, the strict division between the family budget and the budget of the enterprise, the rationalisation of law and the development of the monetary economy—and to have stressed the importance of not neglecting or under-estimating the significance of religion, both for the employer and for the worker.

2. THE EMPLOYER'S ETHICS

Let us consider the employer or capitalist entrepreneur first. He is characterised by a new view of work with its origin in religion, in this case Calvinism. By this term, Weber did not mean the form of Christianity advocated by Calvin himself, but that accepted and transformed by the different Puritan sects deriving from his teaching, in particular the Pietists, Methodists and Baptists. Weber insisted on two points here which his interpreters have tended frequently to neglect, with the result that they have quite easily been able to find fault with his argument. On the one hand, Weber has pointed out that his sources were not the theoretical writings of professional theologians, but those of pastors and ministers of the people who had a great influence on the practical lives and moral behaviour of believers.[9] On the other hand, these early capitalists did not, Weber insisted, come from the upper strata of the population, but from the middle classes and the farming class. These classes revolutionised the economic pattern found in high society, although this revolution was not brought about without difficulties or without hostility. It was also these classes that gave rise to what is known as the bourgeois—or middle-class—morality, in other words, the Puritan spirit.[10] We have therefore to see, on the basis of these statements, how Calvinism inspired a new view of work through its new view of ethics. In this, at least three aspects can be distinguished.

1. Asceticism. There have been various forms of asceticism in other world religions, but the asceticism of the medieval monk is special, because it always had in it the seed of rationalisation which was to develop later. I shall not stress in this article the theme of asceticism in medieval monasticism that Weber analysed again and again. What I would like to emphasise, however, is that the medieval monk not only favoured contemplation as a means of glorifying God—he also regarded work as a way of honouring God. Work was not seen as a form of resignation or as a vital necessity, but as a voluntary and rational discipline. Calvinism also revived this asceticism, but transformed it by placing it at the service of the theory of election. It was no longer characteristic of men and women who fled the world and lived in monasteries and convents, but of those who lived and worked *in* the world. Taking Sebastian Franck as his example, Weber estimated that the really profound importance of the Calvinist Reformation was to make a monk of every Christian during his lifetime. What Puritan morality condemned, on the basis of purely religious presuppositions, was, in Weber's view, being satisfied with possessions, delight in wealth, the temptations of the flesh and luxury, and idleness, in other words, a greedy and dishonest consumption of the world's goods. This morality has led to an accumulation of the fruits of man's labour which must therefore be used for purposes other than immediate gratification. 'Capital', Weber said' 'is created by asceticism in the form of forced saving. It is obvious that the obstacles preventing the consumption of acquired goods favoured their productive use as capital to be invested.'[11] What can, after all, be done with money that one has earned but cannot spend on one's pleasures? It can only be reinvested in the enterprise in order to develop it.

2. Calling. The idea of calling or vocation was known before the Reformation. The only novelty introduced by the Reformers was to apply it to work, by making man's trade or profession a calling. From that time onwards, then, under the religious name of 'calling' (*Beruf*), work became a task imposed on man by God and success in one's trade or profession became a sign of election. Thus, unlike work according to the

view that prevailed in the ancient world and the Middle Ages, labour now had the status of an ethical value and came to be known as a 'duty' or a 'moral obligation'.[12] A total change took place, in other words, in man's concept of work at the time of the Reformation. Until the Reformation, work had been no more than an elemental demand, a necessity and a worry. From the Reformation onwards, it acquired the dignity of a fundamental ethical concept. Even if he acquired a fortune, man still had to give himself over to the daily task, since a moral failure was also a failure to observe God's commandment. It was no longer enough simply to conform outwardly to the Church's requirements, by almsgiving, for example, or by good works, in order to be assured of one's salvation. The only way to earn one's salvation was by working and by not going counter to God's call. God had, the Reformers were convinced, made us the stewards of the goods that he had entrusted to us. By becoming a calling, work tended to become an end in itself.

3. Riches and poverty. With the evangelical counsels in mind, the medieval Church condemned wealth and exalted poverty and even begging. (The evidence of the latter is to be found in the favour with which the mendicant orders were viewed.) Puritanism led to a change in this attitude. Not only was there a demand for social legislation[13]—there was also a need to suppress the opprobrium that accompanied the possession of wealth. Had Christ himself not condemned the servant who failed to add to the talent that his master had entrusted to him? Riches were only evil if they were placed at the service of base, irrational passions. They were not evil if they were in accordance with the demands of ethics and the calling to be stewards of God's goods.[14] Weber noted that 'to the extent that wealth is the crown of the achievement of man's professional duty, it is not only morally permitted, but also effectively prescribed'.[15] Referring to Baxter, Barclay and others, he said: 'It was not a question of imposing mortifications on those who possessed great wealth; all that had to be done was to ensure that their goods were put to necessary and useful ends',[16] since wealth could be providential if, thanks to increasing production, it led to the greatest good of the greatest possible number. In any case, the greatest wealth could not exempt man from his moral duty to work. Weber summarised this new idea in the following way: 'The usefulness of a trade or profession and the approval that God gives to it are measured firstly according to morality, secondly according to the importance of the goods that it has for the community and thirdly—and this third point is, in practice, the most important—according to the economic advantage that it brings. For, if the God whom the Puritan sees at work in all the circumstances of his life shows to one of his elect an opportunity to make a profit, he does it intentionally. The good Christians must respond to this appeal.'[17]

3. THE WORKER'S ETHICS

We will now consider the position of the worker, a question which has up till now received very little attention from the commentators, although Weber devoted several pages to it and there are frequent references to it in all his works. It would seem that their view of this question has in some way been obscured by Weber's argument about the entrepreneurial class and they have consequently neglected the rest. In an attempt to rectify this imbalance, I would point to three aspects of the worker's ethics.

1. As we have already seen, it is hardly possible to speak of a proletariat before the coming of modern capitalism. In other words, both concepts must be kept in mind if we are to understand the social consequences to which Weber draws attention and especially the question of rural depopulation and increasing urbanisation. Since the coming of capitalism, Western society has been involved in an entirely new process of development, since the new morality, which is specifically bourgeois, has led to some gains and some losses for the working class as well. What is quite certain is that the social question was no longer one of begging or almsgiving, in other words, of charity, but of social progress.

2. The popular preachers of the period did not address only the entrepreneurs, who, as Weber has pointed out, were for the most part 'parvenus'.[18] They also preached to those who were to become the workers of capitalist society. In this context, Weber commented: 'The modern worker's practice of regarding his work as a calling has become as characteristic of him as the employer's corresponding attitude towards the acquisition of wealth characterises his class'.[19] He also developed this idea of the connection between religious conviction and the capitalist mentality that is worth quoting in full here: 'The middle-class *entrepreneur* believed that he was especially blessed with the fullness of God's grace at least for as long as he stayed within the limits of formally correct behaviour, his conduct continued to be beyond reproach and he shocked no one by what he did with his wealth. This conviction enabled him to look after his financial interests. Indeed, he regarded it as his duty to do so. In addition, because of the strength of religious asceticism, he had at his disposal workers who were sober, conscientious and unusually industrious and who identified themselves with their work, which they regarded as a God-given aim in life. Finally, this ascetic religious conviction was powerful enough to reassure him that the unequal distribution of this world's goods was in accordance with a special decree of Providence, which, with these differences and with special grace, has aims that are not revealed to us'.'[20] Weber also points out, elsewhere in his book, that the persecution that the Methodist workers had to suffer in the eighteenth century at the hands of their fellow-workers was at least partly

attributable to 'their excessive good will towards work'.[21] He also noted in this context that the female workers, who had been given a Pietistic religious education, were more open to the new economic opportunities.[22]

3. It was not long before the problem of the fate of the worker was discussed in Calvinist terms of the poverty of the people that was necessary to keep them obedient to God. Referring to such authors as T. Adams and Pieter de la Court, Weber showed that the question of wages was given a religious meaning, namely that people only worked if they were poor and remained poor.[23] It was observed, however, that very low wages did not produce tangible results because they were an obstacle to an expansion in quality of capitalist enterprises and were insufficient to lead to intensive labour. It was also found that, if returns were to be increased, the workers had to have a strong sense of responsibility. The religious education that had transformed work into a calling in fact brought about this sense of responsibility, as we have seen in the case of the Methodist and Pietistic workers. This is precisely why Weber insisted that we should recognise, on the basis of pastoral practice, the correlation that initially at least existed between, on the one hand, the personal quality of the worker and that of the employer (who in any case had usually come from the same social environment) and, on the other, the religious conviction that provided their underlying moral attitude.

4. A NEW PERSPECTIVE

It has not been my aim, in suggesting this rather unusual interpretation of Weber's views about work and religion, to refute the thinking of other commentators. All that I have wanted to do is to make a few corrections and additions to the existing analysis of Weber's work, however difficult it may be to do this in a short article. I may have done no more than provide a few indicators pointing to a better understanding of his work.

Two common criticisms of Weber's thought have above all to be answered. The first is that he has misrepresented Calvin's teaching. Weber, however, was never primarily concerned with theory in this context. He was only concerned with the sects that had been produced by Calvinism and with their pastoral practice. With reference to the reformers who originated these sects, he said, for example: 'In their lives and activities, they were exclusively preoccupied with the salvation of souls. Their ethical aims and the practical manifestations of their teachings were all rooted in this exclusive preoccupation and were no more than the consequences of certain purely religious motives. That is why we should expect the effects of the Reformation on human society to be, to a very great extent and, from our particular point of view, even preponderantly, the unforeseen consequences of the work of the Reformers and not the consequences that they had anticipated and wanted. These consequences were often very remote from everything that the Reformers had striven to bring about and were sometimes even diametrically opposed to their original intentions.'[24] There is a great danger of misunderstanding the essential meaning of Weber's work on Protestant ethics and capitalism if what he called the paradox of consequences in his epistomology is not borne constantly in mind.

The second criticism that is often made of Weber is that an economic system is too closely associated in his thinking with a religious doctrine. Weber anticipated this criticism and insisted that his argument only applied to one form of capitalism, namely modern enterprise capitalism. He did not have all forms of capitalism at all periods of history in mind. In the course of time, the *entrepreneurs* who were inspired by Calvinism and who had become powerful frequently tended to deny the religious ethos that had originally inspired them, especially if they had been able to adapt themselves to high society and to become members of the nobility in those countries where this was possible.

To conclude this article, I would like to quote once again from Weber's book on the Protestant ethos and the spirit of capitalism. In a passage in which he explains quite frankly the significance of his work, he says: 'What I have tried to do is to distinguish, from the mass of historical factors contributing to the development of our modern civilisation in its specific orientation towards this world, that element that can be traced back to religious factors and to clarify it. My aim has been only to distinguish, from the many aspects that characterise that civilisation, those that may suitably be imputed to the Reformation as a historical cause. In doing this, I have had to reject the idea that the Reformation can be inferred as a "historical necessity" from economic changes. The very opposite is true and there are very many historical circumstances which cannot be included within any "economic law" or be explained in terms of economics—I am thinking here especially of purely political processes—and which must have combined to help the newly created Churches to survive. On the other hand, it would be impossible to insist on the irrational and doctrinaire claim that the spirit of capitalism . . . could *only* be the result of certain Reformation influences or to go so far as to state that, as an economic system, capitalism was created by the Reformation. The simple fact that many important forms of capitalist organisation are much older than the Reformation is sufficient to refute this claim.'[25]

Translated by David Smith

Notes

1. The author quotes from his own translation of Weber's work: *Ethique protestante et esprit du capitalisme* 2nd ed. (Paris 1965) p. 143.

2. *Ibid.* pp. 78-79.

3. *Gesammelte Aufsätze zur Religionssoziologie* 4th ed. (Tübingen 1947) I, p. 448.

4. *Wirtschaft und Gesellschaft*; French edition *Economie et Société* (Paris 1971) I, p. 144.

5. *Ibid*. p. 156.

6. *Ethique protestante* p. 18.

7. *Ibid.* p. 20.

8. *Ibid*. p. 21.

9. *Ibid.* p. 218.

10. *Ibid* pp. 239-240; see also p. 67.

11. *Ibid.* p. 237.

12. *Ibid.* p. 79. Weber notes in passing that it is interesting that this concept of work and capital developed not in Italy, the centre of the world's money markets, but in the middle of the Pennsylvanian forests, where there were almost no industrial enterprises and banking was only just beginning. He adds: 'It would be meaningless to speak in this context of a reflection of the material conditions on to the ideal superstructure.'

13. *Ibid.* p. 245.

14. Weber quotes here an astonishing statement by Baxter, pp. 217-218, who showed that, as soon as wealth is seen as God's will, it is stripped of the inhibitions within which it had hitherto been held captive by religion.

15. *Ethique protestante* p. 218.

16. *Ibid.* p. 235.

17. *Ibid.* p. 217.

18. *Ibid.* p. 67.

19. *Ibid.* pp. 246-247.

20. *Ibid.* pp. 243-244.

21. *Ibid.* p. 65.

22. *Ibid.* p. 64.

23. *Ibid.* pp. 62 and 244.

24. *Ibid.* p. 105.

25. *Ibid.* pp. 106-107.

PART II

Analysis of Actual Situations

François Houtart and Geneviève Lemercinier

Religion and the Reproduction of Social Structures

Catholicism and the Structure of Caste in an Area of South India

ACCEPTANCE that religion plays a major part in the recreation of the patterns of social relationships implies its recognition as a symbolic way of thinking; it forms a frame of reference which, at one and the same time, draws out and explains those characteristics of the group which determine what it is in itself and the manner in which it interacts with other social groups.

Having been able to verify how well founded one such hypothesis was in connection with Hinduism in South India,[1] we wondered whether it would be possible to explain the reason for the penetration of Catholicism into the greater part of the Tamil-Nadu countryside from the sixteenth century onwards (The Missions of Madurai) and the reasons for the social consequences of those conversions both as they happened in the past and today. The area is still affected socially by caste divisions which, even if it does not entirely organise the economic field, still has a major influence on the apportionment of activities between groups, in the exercise of power, in the way they think about the world and even in the allocation of space.[2]

1. THE SOCIAL CONDITIONS AND CONSEQUENCES OF THE PENETRATION OF CATHOLICISM INTO THE TAMIL-NADU COUNTRYSIDE (SIXTEENTH-NINETEENTH CENTURIES)

The supremacy of the Pandyans was evident even when the Greeks and Romans were carrying on commercial activities with South India, a little before the first millennium, and they were followed some centuries later by the Chinese and then by the Arabs. The importance of this merchant economy was such that it formed the basis of a particular social system which Marx called the Asiatic method of production.

The central political power was founded on the basis of exchange arrangements between the different tribes—they were assured of military protection if they, in turn, supplied tribute in marketable produce or in food necessary for the military class. In one such situation the political power did not intervene in the internal social organisation of the tribes, except at the level of what use was to be made of any surplus: it introduced them into a market economy and took a part of their produce. Each of the tribes kept its internal autonomy based on family relationships, its system of collective administration and the symbolic vision of life which expressed its links with nature (such as spirits both evil and good) and its social unity (the divinity of the clan, the totem and its ancestors).

In the area of Ramnad, to the south of Madurai, which was originally inhabited by two clans, the Maravars, hunters of small game and the Paravars, who were pearl fishermen, this process particularly affected the former. The Maravars had little to offer in a market economy for many years and so made up the great part of the army of the King's Madurai and then that of other monarchs. The area was opened up to groups in search of space who belonged to neighbouring tribes, the Vellalars, farmers from the area of Tanjore, the Kallars from the neighbourhood of Madurai, the Chanars from the West and some pre-Dravidian groups from the mountainous region of the Ghats.

From a religious point of view in this area the penetration of Hinduism was slow. Certainly from the first period of the development of Madurai the presence of a political class who disposed of the surplus drew religious representatives to the city—as much Brahmin, as Buddhist and Jain monks, and in the same way attracted intellectuals, poets and craftsmen. It was only from the tenth century onwards that the Brahmin group began to dominate.

In the area of Ramnad, although few in number, they established themselves in the agricultural zones as the only ones capable of supplying the levy from the produce of the soil. They built themselves temples and introduced a religious pattern which their status as political-religious representatives enabled them to do. It involved a division of society into four *varnas*. Only the first two levels, the Brahmins and the Khastryas (the political caste) were considered to be Hindu castes. The Sudras (the manual workers) and the Vaisyas (the merchants) were excluded by the fact of the manual nature of their work. Once the system had been imposed upon the society of South India it produced a hierarchy of social groups according to their occupation and their ethnic origin. In rural areas, the Vellalars, who employed aboriginal farm labourers (the Pallars and the Parayars) were considered as a superior Hindu caste. The Chanars and the Kollars, who were Dravidian but were not manual agricultural workers, were given the caste status which excluded them from participation in religious activities because of the impurity of their work. The Maravars (who lived as soldiers or as brigands) and the Pallavars (fishermen) were ignored in the social structure. As for the Pallars and the Parayars who were non-Dravidian and worked on inferior tasks, they were considered 'the untouchables'.

So it is into this socio-cultural context that Christianity entered. These social and cultural constraints not only influenced the content of belief and the way in which the religion was expressed but also the method of Church organisation. The groups kept some specific traditional activities which played a key role in the definition of their identity. From the religious point of view the syncretistic features combined the double function of regulating the relationships within the natural order and preserving the unity of the group. Because of the hostile nature of the conditions which made the area of little interest to the political powers, the development of productive forces was very feeble there. Besides, one of the reasons for the success of Christianity was that it appeared to be able to act effectively on such natural conditions as illness, epidemic, drought, flood, etc. This aspect of its work, though widespread through all groups, was expressed differently from one group to another.

The *Annual* letters of the Jesuits reveal the importance of the cult of the patron saint which had replaced the traditional divinity. To him vows were made for miracles which were received, nothing was too rich to use for adorning his statue or for his festival cart. In principle, the saint only favoured the members of the caste of that place. There were, however, certain pilgrimage centres which drew people every year from all the groups of the same caste. Among the Chanars, for example, St James the Greater was the patron saint of the caste. His miracles, however, were worked through the mediation of the tree which had formerly been the totem and now was supposed to be the place where he lived. Among the Panavars the water which had been blessed by St Francis Xavier had miraculous properties. The analysis of these practices taken as a whole show that what is happening is that some elements of Christianity are being substituted for traditional religious patterns. This was, moreover, favoured by the official religious representatives.[3] The Christian villages greatly honoured their patron St Michael. The fact that he was a warrior reminded them that formerly their caste had supplied the infantry for the royal armies. The missionaries laid down as a condition for receiving baptism that they should renounce theft which was a traditional activity among the Maravars. The latter also got into the habit of delaying baptism until they were *in articulo mortis*. This allowed the so-called

Christians to marry quite legally with non-Christians in accordance with caste regulations. All the same the missionaries celebrated Mass among them and their children were catechised. Far from unifying the different social groups of the converted Indians by adapting itself in this way (a necessary condition to its adoption), Christianity continued to supply cultural support for the reproduction of caste as specific groups.

2. THE STRUCTURE OF THE CASTE AND THE EXPRESSION OF CONTEMPORARY RELIGION

With the introduction of the capitalist methods of production through the influence of the English colonisation the local structure hardly changed. It was the *zamindars* who effected the connection between the colonial power and the local populations through the Indian Rajahs whether small or great. The system of bonded labour was pursued on the estates of the land owners who themselves paid the taxes. The villages remained separate units, independently organised, with the caste system always deciding the division of physical labour and each person's position in the social order. Only with the coming of agrarian reform after independence do you see some change being introduced. A large number of small landowners were created developing some small businesses in subsistence economy run by the people themselves. In 1971, they represented in the east of the district of Ramnad (the area studied) more than 50 per cent of the whole. But the farm workers also continued to exist; they formed more than 20 per cent.

One small industry has been established in the area (mainly brick-making) but it has scarcely affected the social structure. Each year a certain number of agricultural workers who are outside the caste system go to Madras to work as labourers during the season when there is no work in the countryside. But they return to the village afterwards. Education has at last penetrated some way enabling certain castes particularly to occupy some clerical and administrative posts. It is in this way that the Nadars (formerly the Chanars) are set on a very clear road to social progress. Thus economic status and caste status do not totally coincide. It is evidently the economic factor which regulates the new relationship in productive work. It is necessary to add, moreover, that the salary system has slowly replaced that of bonded labour—though not entirely so.

We shall now choose some groups which are characteristic of the area studied taking a closer look at their situation, their work, their religious expressions and practices.

The Vellalars

The Vellalars are farmers and are considered to be high caste. In 1975 they had the highest proportion of land (small properties mainly of less than five hectares). Their representation on the *panchayats* (the council) is predominant. Politically they are, in general near to the DMK (a nationalist Dravidian party which is anti-Brahmin). It is an active and enterprising group. For example they employ chemical fertiliser to a far greater extent than others, agriculture has become a subsidiary activity for many of them who have taken up commercial work and teaching—especially for Catholics in the educational system of the Church. They are to be found as catechists and as parochial officers. An important section of the local clergy come from this caste. The Church as an institution is an important channel for their social ascent.

They are also marked by a somewhat over-emphasised individualism. The clergy complain about them and although they are attached to religion, even that is ritualistic. Their level of Sunday observance is very high. They have a festival of their own, prepared by the system of *mandakapadi*, in which each family takes responsibility for one day of the feast, but contrary to the other caste, there is no communal preparation.

Among their acts of devotion, there are first the ancient ones inherited from the Portuguese which took the place of the worship of the Hindu gods. Thus, St Thomas the hermit is invoked for the harvest and St Sebastian for healings. St Michael is the protector of the villages (similar to the protective Hindu gods pictured on a horse). A more recent act of devotion is that to Our Lady of Perpetual Succour; she is linked to economic or academic success and also to the obtaining of a good marriage partner. She scarcely exists in the lower castes or among the outcasts. Indeed in Asia (in Sri Lanka and the Philippines) for example this is usually only an urban act of devotion.[4]

Recourse to astrologers is frequent, above all to get an indication of the propitious days for commercial transactions, for new types of work and for marriages, etc. No commercial deal will be enacted on a Friday after sunset. The belief in charms is very widespread in the case of illness.

The Maravars

In the past the Maravars were the soldiers of the Pandyan and Chola kings, then they became nomads and highwaymen by force of circumstances. They have turned to agriculture since the end of British colonisation. Their past history is still very alive for them. The main deity of the Hindu Maravars is Sangeli Karuppan, a deified hero. The *Nadu Kal*, which is a commemorative stone, is the object of a daily ritual and commemorates great warriors. The Sunday observance of the Catholics is very weak and they have little contact with the clergy—contrary to the Vellalars. Their festival is the harvest (*Pongal*) and it is St Anthony the hermit who is celebrated. Community games take place which are specific to the caste. The devotion moves mainly between two poles—St Anthony the hermit for harvest and livestock and Our Lady of Perpetual Succour for a successful existence. Two others must be mentioned—St John of Britto who was the means of their conversion and Father Leveil, a missionary at the beginning of the century who is celebrated for his power to bring rain and to keep away the plague from the fields. They also turned to astrologers, they consult the *Kodangis* (the fortune-tellers) and as they believe in evil spirits they practise certain propitiatory rights. From an ethical point of view one notes also a certain sexual laxity.

The Nadars

After having been involved in the maintenance of transport in the tributary areas, the Chanars, as they were called until recently, turned to the extraction of the juice of the palm tree and the coconut tree. These activities do not put them very high in the caste system. At the moment the group is enjoying a quite spectacular rise in social status through the influence of their clerical and administrative work: the public services, commerce and finance. Because of this they have gradually changed their name to the Nadars. There is a strong caste cohesion and a highly developed system of mutual aid.

Among the Catholics Sunday worship is well attended and the participation in morning and evening prayer is quite good. Their specific festival is prepared by a committee nominated by the council of the caste. In order that it should be an outstanding occasion, they take no account of the expenditure involved. Significant amounts are distributed on this occasion in alms. The main devotional activity is directed towards St James because, 'as a son of thunder', he is able to cause rain and because he opposes dishonesty. Because of this the village council is held opposite the church containing his statue and it is said that those who lie will die while vomiting blood. Prayers are also offered to St Anthony and St Michael on the subject of dishonest people. Mention should be made too of St Anne and St Joachim. Prayers are said to them for happy births or by wives having a sick husband. St Francis Xavier and James de Rossi and a Jesuit ministry called *Sinna Saveriar* (that is the little Xavier) are also objects of devotion. They also turn to Hindu divinities where it seems that Catholic rights are ineffective. In particular they pray to Maramman for protection against smallpox. As for consulting astrologers, it is general practice to use them for fixing marriage dates and other new activities.

The Paravars

The Paravars have always been placed outside the caste structure because of their fishing activities. They live along the coast of South India. As in all fishing communities, their academic level is very low (because they go to sea at any early age) and the sexual taboos are very strict. They believe, for instance, that if a wife commits adultery while a husband is at sea he will perish while he is there. A large section of them were converted to Catholicism at the time when they were looking for protection against the Muslims. St Francis Xavier was one of those who baptised them. Religious observance is very weak and almost non-existent among the men. No one arranges morning prayer in these villages and few have a catechist. St James is the centre of their devotional life. He is thought to protect fishermen at sea and to ensure good catches. A number of miracles and apparitions are attributed to him. But St Anthony of Padua is also honoured. They pray to him for success in fishing, for marriages, in legal cases, for protection against cholera and smallpox. They look to him also for help against thieves and they seek his help in finding stolen objects. At his shrine children are consecrated and for this they have to have their heads shaved. The festivals are organised in honour of these two saints. The village elders decide on the tax which must be paid by each family to their organisations. The expenses are very heavy; in one village the expenses for one festival came to 12 000 rupees. But the very cost increases the prestige of the group. The devotions to St Michael and to the sacred heart (which takes place on the first Friday of the month) should also be noted. The former is the one who protects them against the devil (Pilli Sooniam) and at the same time against illness and enemies. As far as the devotion to Our Lady of Perpetual Succour is concerned she assures them of success in marketing their fish, in examinations, in finding work or a partner and in guaranteeing a happy birth.

They frequently turn to other gods. They make offerings at the temple of Murugan, at the time of epidemics they turn to Marriaman. At the time of the death of an infant who is very young they attribute the misfortune to Muni the evil spirit who has attacked the child and they pierce the ear of the child who is next in age in order to protect it from the same evil. They have a fertility cult in the area of a tree situated in the centre of the village, etc.

The Parayars

The Parayars are outcasts (pariahs). They are pre-Dravidian in origin and this fact places them, like all clans of this kind, at the bottom of the social ladder. They are an exploited group; agricultural workers, grave diggers, dustmen, all ways of life which the Hindus regard as being highly polluted. For a long time they had to build their huts outside the village and even now they often have their wells and cemeteries there. Completely fixed in the social structure they have now no hope of getting out of it. The Catholics among them are scarcely practising. Their work does not leave them very much leisure time and some of them migrate for seasonal industrial work in Madras. They are misunderstood by Catholics from other castes and often they are put in a separate part of the church. Even the clergy make them objects of criticism because of their feeble participation in religious activities and their customary drinking, sport and sexual licence. The festival is full of activities. It begins in the evening with a procession of the statutes of the various saints such as Our Lady, St James, St Anthony mounted on carts and accompanied by drums, fireworks and Bengal lights. They are invoked for rain. The procession is followed by theatrical performances or a film. In the morning after Mass there is a new procession made up of those who have made promises to the Saints. This event ends up with dancing, sport and sexual debauchery. At Christmas the festival is celebrated with sugar (*sakkaraithirunal*). And at midnight twelve kilogrammes of sugar are distributed.

The central devotion is to the Virgin as she appeared in various places such as at Velankani (the place of pilgrimage to Mary for the people of Tamil Nadu), at Lourdes or Fatima. She is their principal protector; she chases away the evil spirits (Muni), above all from women who are possessed, and heals children and sick husbands (the women offer their *thali*, the necklace which symbolises their matrimonial union). The Holy Family, St Anthony and St John of Britto are also venerated. St John the Evangelist is the protector of the villages which have been studied but that is because of a missionary initiative. Many Hindus of the same caste prayed to the Virgin because she is considered more powerful than their gods. The Catholics share in the festivities of the Parayar Hindus and also consult *Kodangis* and astrologers and fortune-tellers. They do not however seek to worship the Hindu gods.

This is a brief description of some of the forms of religious expression among some of the characteristic castes. Now we must inquire into their social significance.

The first thing which strikes us about these religious means of expression is the function that certain of them fulfil to represent relationships to nature. Into this category come all those rites and devotions which have to do with protection against natural hazards or with obtaining favours linked with what they produce in agriculture or fishing and with health. Certain religious activities continue even though there is no longer any reason for their existence—such as prayers for the saints who ward off cholera or smallpox. But it is true to say that these ills are still very much alive in the collective memory. The persistence of these practices can be explained by the fact that the area is only on the fringe of economic development and that that situation also helps to reinforce the natural explanation of a certain number of the aspects of social relationships, such as festivals and devotions to particular saints.

So it appears that forms of religious expression such as festivals and devotions to particular saints act to maintain group identity. They form a specific pattern in each caste and are linked to a situation in the social and economic structure. Among Vellalars it is a matter of expressing that the group finds its identity in its dominance. Among the Nadars the religious elements reinforce group cohesion by emphasising its rise in social status; among the Paravars the religious event simply breaks the daily round of life without reference to an identity which indeed they would prefer to see disappear.

We recall the fact that the social structure involving the payment of tribute was built at base on the pattern of social relationships between a central power and a number of local units which were strongly self-governing. We noted that this pattern did not normally exist in a capitalist society where the whole system of social relationships is determined by the salary system. Since the caste system no longer determines this pattern, what reinforces the identity of castes and their respective positions must, therefore, be linked with a social system of production that is now a thing of the past. But that does not mean that the caste solidarity does not have some important function in the contemporary situation. In effect, on the one hand the capitalist economic organisation has not penetrated deeply into the area and in consequence there is much to be gained in maintaining the cultural codes of behaviour as they were in the past. On the other hand the fragmentation into castes prevents the development of class solidarity even among the small-scale peasants or agricultural workers. Religion (which in our case is as much a matter of Catholicism as of Hinduism) contributes in this way to the reproduction of the traditional social relationship in a situation where they are useful in a peripheral capitalism. It is certainly not its only function but it is important to take into account as an explanatory factor when a weak development of the productive forces combine with the marginal economy.[5]

Translated by T. J. W. Sampson

Notes

1. See G. Lemercinier *Religion et idéologie au Kerala; Modes de production et fonctions sociales de la religion* (Louvain-la-neuve 1977) Roneo-typed report, I, Part 3, Ch. 1.

2. See *A Socio-religious Analysis of the East Ramnad District (Tamilnadu)* (Dindigul 1977), available in polycopied form at the Centre de Recherches Socio-Religieuses, Catholic University of Louvain, p. 524.

3. See L. Besse S.J. *La Mission du Madure, Historique de ses pangous* (Trinchinopoly, Imprimerie de la Mission Catholique, 1954) p. 256. In these missionary reports which were sent to Rome notes like the following can be found: In parish X there was a count of 653 miracles worked by the power of the holy water of St Francis Xavier blessed by Father Y. At Z, the priest recorded 119 miracles obtained through the water and 21 through the tree of St James.

4. Similar acts of devotion occur both in Hinduism and Buddhism. It is, for example, the same for Sankara and Sri Lanka.

5. The study carried out in the district of Ramnad was done on the initiative of Jesuits who were directed to carry out social work in this area. It gave them an opportunity to redefine their pastoral and social aims in which, among other matters, they gave priority to the defence of the rights of the Parayans and the Pallars (the untouchables).

Francisco Rolim

Religion and Poverty: Brazil

1. INTRODUCTION

OUR PURPOSE is to focus on the relationship between poverty and religion within the framework of a particular historical situation. This does not mean that we shall be considering these subjects only from a factual point of view. A theoretical approach is needed, since it regulates the interpretation of reality. Thus, by historical situation, we mean Brazilian society in its contemporary capitalist stage, that is, since 1930. Its organisation is based on the system of production, distribution and consumption. This implies a difference in relation to the preceding system, which was also capitalist. Externally, a number of international events (and particularly the great depression of world capitalism) had far-reaching repercussions on the Brazilian economy. Internally, the national economy is moving from being that of a country exporting primary products and importing manufactured products to that of a country with differentiated industrial production directed to the internal market. This did not, however, occur without profound effects at the economic, the political and the social levels.

At the economic level, the incipient industrialisation created in the vacuum left by the export/import system was gradually replaced by a diversified industrialisation which tends to form the economic basis of the new stage. Such a situation will tend to make for a gradual appearance of urban factory workers, for a greater growth of the service and commercial sectors and for an imbalance between the demand for skilled workers and an inadequate supply. The process of urbanisation and its acceleration in the years after 1950, without a corresponding increase in industrialisation, caused such industries as did already exist to absorb as best they could the workers who poured into the towns, and particularly the larger ones.

At the political level, a social reorganisation set in spontaneously and led to the breaking of both internal and external ties. For example, the dominant agrarian oligarchy connected with the export sectors broke up and simultaneously a number of conditions were created for the emergence of urban employers. Popular sectors appeared as a new power, putting pressure on the government and compelling the transition, according to Gino Germani, from a limited democracy to an enlarged democracy.

At the social level, popular strata appeared as objects of government consideration and they demanded better conditions of life. They constituted a significant element in the policy of the masses in opposition to the restrictive policy of the parties. They represent something new at a socio-political level; they want to find a place in democracy and they are destined to participate more effectively in the redemocratisation that has been taking place since 1945.

These popular strata, who have been present at different social levels, expanding over the years from the most developed to the less developed areas, do not agree with the new phase of Brazilian capitalism, but they are structurally built into it.

2. URBANISATION AND POPULAR SECTORS

Two kinds of links between urbanisation and socio-economic development allow us to identify different sorts of urbanisation in the present and in the previous stage of capitalism. The first stage of urbanisation, before 1930, was characterised by the subordination of the demographic increase of towns to the spontaneous increase of the industrial sector that emerged in the vacuum created by the export system, as well as to the commercial activities and the supply of commodities in towns. In the second stage, the relationship was inverted: in the contemporary stage of capitalism, urbanisation dominates new industrialisation. This predominance seems to be a characteristic of the socio-economic development that is based on diversified industrialisation. Thus, the urbanisation that predominates over industrialisation takes shape as a sub-process of development, tending to be autonomous and producing a new phase of social organisation. In this case, we are concerned not only with urbanisation in the sense of a simple demographic growth of towns. As a sub-process of the system of production, distribution and consumption, it tends to develop internal industrial production and to create diversified and complementary industries. In his classical definition of urbanism as a form of life, a concept that has become well known, Wirth pointed out the relevance of urban ethos and its inherent values and its own rules, establishing a psycho-social dimension differentiating it from non-urban areas. According to this idea, urbanisation is a dimension deeper than the simple quantitative increase of population in towns in so far as it is characterised by a particular style of life. Nevertheless we think it is necessary to release this conception from its restriction to towns and to enlarge it to embrace the larger concept of general urbanisation.

Two concepts constitute the basis of this idea: effect-demonstration and 'mobilisation'. The first concept is a matter of the influence of towns upon non-urban areas as seen at different levels and grades of consumption, imitation and processes of social organisation. In contrast, the second concept is a matter of a psycho-social atmosphere conducive to a reflexive and critical, and therefore deliberative, capacity enabling the development of different levels of aspirations and aims, which are distinguishable from and sometimes in opposition to the pre-existing patterns of normative behaviour. Gino Germani suggest that the concept of mobilisation be defined in terms of a 'transition from prescriptive to elective action'. This is spelled out by the author as follows: '(Mobilisation) corresponds to the psycho-sociological process by which groups pass from being immersed in the passivity of the traditional model (the predominance of prescriptive action as a consequence of the accomplishment of inner rules) to acquiring a certain capacity for deliberative behaviour, move on to aspirations different from the ones established by the older pattern, and as a consequence develop a number of political activities. These groups participate in national affairs and their intervention can be expressed in different ways: spontaneous protest movements, open revolutionary explosions, religious movements, political activities inside the parties, participation in elections.'[1]

According to this concept, we can say that urbanisation understood in this way not only as a way of life that extends beyond the geographical boundaries of towns but as a dimension of mobilisation in the sense given by Germani and as a sub-process of the development of the contemporary stage of capitalism, tends to develop the deliberative potential of the masses of the people at all levels of society, including the poorest and lowest classes. If we consider the surroundings of large towns full of people coming from small centres and from rural areas, then in relation to the poorest classes we can say that misery is indeed transported to the towns but we can also say that, step by step, the potential for deliberative behaviour develops too and with it the replacement of the normative patterns that guide passive behaviour. In non-urban areas where mobilisation sets in, the apron strings of passivity are broken. Then the deprived classes wake up to the possibility of deliberative behaviour and this has repercussions at the political level. For until now such popular classes, constituted predominantly by service, commerce, transport and to a lesser extent by factory and rural workers, have been buffeted by the vagaries of the regime and by demagogic popular leaders, and they have been refused a democratic participation in dictatorial regimes.

In the light of all this, we can consider the role that religion plays, by reference to the two main forces in question: on the one hand, the Catholic Church as the bearer of the official religion and the subject of the recent experience of Basic Communities (*Communidades de Base*), and on the other hand the popular religious movements that have expanded recently, that is, Pentecostalism in its Protestant form. On the one side, then, we have the Church and its organisation settled in urban areas since colonial times; on the other side, Pentecostalism born among us in the decade 1910–1920 but which penetrated the masses of the people deeply and which nowadays covers 70 per cent of the evangelicals.

3. RELIGION AND THE MASSES OF THE PEOPLE

Generally speaking, the Church has made very few changes in its ecclesiastical organisation since the early 1930's. This remained the same, that is, it consisted in urban parishes and religious associations guided from on top downwards. Catholic Action movements were undertaken according to European models, they were organised to suit the interests of an élite, and among the workers they did not perceive the basic problems of the Brazilian working classes. On the other hand, the liturgical movements are characterised by intellectuality and rationality and their religious symbolism is dissociated from the popular classes. According to the hierarchy, the mass of the people, mainly the poorest ones, lives submerged in religious ignorance, as measured by the standards of the knowledge of the clergy. The members of this clergy superintended the devotional practices through associations, parishes and schools ruled by ecclesiastics. Religious ceremonies practised by people outside those organisations were regarded as an ensemble of superstitious rituals. The knowledge priests acquired was an obstacle in the way of understanding the religious experience of people.[2]

This experience can, however, be interpreted in an entirely different way. It was such religious feeling that provoked the massive gatherings of popular forces on such occasions as the celebration in honour of Our Lady of the Apparition in Rio de Janeiro, the Eucharistic Congress and popular missions. The clergy may indeed have controlled these manifestations of popular religious feeling but these did have the latent function of stating the power of the Church in the presence of a new social order. In this connection, we may, generally speaking, admit that the poorest classes of the population did not get any particular attention from the Church, which was mainly concerned with the upper middle classes of the rural oligarchy and the urban bourgeoisie. This is shown in statistics of mass-going collected in over a hundred towns of Brazil during the 1960's. In towns with 100 000 inhabitants or more there was a low ratio of church-goers; in more developed areas, the figures were as follows: In Santos/S. Vicente, 12 per cent; Ribeirão Preto, 22 per cent; Nova Iguaçú, near Rio de Janeiro, 6 per cent. In northern less developed areas, the figures were as follows: Fortaleza, 31 per cent; Campina Grande, 22 per cent. Other smaller areas show variations between 15 per cent and 32 per cent. The higher percentages refer to people who suffered fewer vicissitudes. More than half of the people who attend Sunday services are unemployed. The Church's official worship did not succeed in penetrating the world of work. 30 per cent to 35 per cent of the working people belong to the middle and upper sectors of commerce and service, and the number of semi-skilled and/or unskilled workers present in Church is extremely insignificant. Even in industrial areas the number of workers attending Church was low. As the service sector is predominant in relation to the labour sector, even in more developed areas it is only to be expected that it should be represented more significantly at mass. But the great majority of semi-skilled workers, who are significant in all areas (people like tailors, shoe-makers, stone-masons, mechanics, etc.), do not attend Church services. The number of illiterate or semi-literate people present in Church is another point: in the less developed areas—Foraleza, 7 per cent; Campina Grande, 8 per cent; Caruarú, 9 per cent; in the more developed areas: Nova Iguaçu, 0·5 per cent; Santos/S. Vicente, 4 per cent; Ribeirão Preto, 5 per cent.[3] In areas dominated by prescriptive patterns of behaviour the rate of illiteracy is even greater. We have to pay particular attention to the environs of large and medium size cities. They are inhabited by people who have low income, a low level of education, few professional qualifications, and live in poor houses. Such areas, which constitute a ring of poverty, are not actually influenced by the official worship of the Church. In this way a religious vacuum was created, free from Church control and open to the impact of other credos. Pentecostalism found good conditions in which to penetrate and expand.

In 1910, the first Pentecostal Church of the Christian Congregation of Brazil (*Congregação Cristã do Brasil*), later renamed the Christian Congregation in Brazil (*Congregação Cristã do Brasil*) was set up on the edge of the city of São Paulo. In 1911, the Assembly of God (*Assembleia de Deus*) opened its first church in Belém, in the north of Brazil. We can say that Pentecostalism put down its roots in the years between 1910 and 1930. The years after 1930 witnessed the expansion of Pentecostalism. Some idea of its development may be gained from the following figures: in 1930 Pentecostals (including the Christian Congregation—*Congregação Cristã*) included 25 per cent of the evangelicals; in 1950 some 51 per cent; and at present an estimated 70 per cent of all evangelicals. The most powerful branches of the Brazilian Pentecostal evangelical churches (now more than sixty) are: the Christian Congregation (*Congregação Cristã*), the Assembly of God (*Assembleia de Deus*), Foursquare Gospel (*Evangelho Quadrangular*) and Brazil for Christ (*I Brasil para Cristo*). The last one was founded by a Brazilian man who had been a member of some of the different Pentecostal churches. Assembly of God is the most widely-spread of all these principal branches. Its first church was founded in 1911, in the north of the country. From the north it spread to other districts, North, Southeast and South, so that by 1940 it was already represented in all the states and national territories. The other principal churches concentrated in the South and the Southeast, but since 1950 they have moved out to the Northeast and the North. All these Pentecostal churches look for support among the poorest classes of the people. There is, however, one exception: the Temple of New Life (*I Templo da Nova Vida*), which has had only a limited growth, is supported by the middle strata of the middle classes.

The growth of Pentecostalism is completely different from the growth of traditional Protestant churches. Between 1960 and 1970 the rate of growth of Pentecostalism was 101 per cent, whilst that of non-Pentecostals was only 49 per cent. During these same years the absolute growth of evangelicals was 1 040 000 to which Pentecostalism contributed to the tune of 70 per cent. The expansion of Pentecostal temples may give us an idea of this growth: in 1910, there were 2; in 1930, 267; in 1950, 1924; in 1970, 11 118. In 1970, 73 per cent of Pentecostals were concentrated in the economically more developed regions of Southeast and the South. But this concentration was already taking place even before 1970, albeit on a lesser scale. The growth and concentration of Evangelicals, mainly the Pentecostals in the more developed areas, induced some social scientists who studied the problem to correlate the growth of Pentecostalism with socio-cultural changes. Using a functional approach, such authors[4] brought out Pentecostalism's function of giving its followers possibilities of social promotion which poor people could not find in society. Looked at in this way, Pentecostal religion prepares its followers for the perpetual changes in society. They accept the concept of anomie, applying it even at the moral level. This kind of approach tells us what Pentecostalism does without actually saying what it consists in. Our own approach is different: we maintain that converts to the Pentecostal faith carry the religious spirit over from elsewhere: 81 per cent are Catholics with a predominantly devotional life.[5] Pentecostalism embraces this pre-existent religiousness, absorbing it and changing its individual form into a collective one. In both public and private worship, during sermons in public squares, believers pray according to their own inspiration. Thus, they become the direct producers of religious products. This is the internal religious structure of Pentecostalism, as characterised by the behaviour of its believers in regard to the products of their religious world, irrespective of whether they are ministers or not. This structural position defines believers as direct producers of the sacral world in a collective dimension. But this religious world is not dissociated from the present stage of capitalism. They are structurally tied together through the social class involved. More than 50 per cent of followers of Pentecostalism are virtually unskilled workers (whereas those who attend Sunday services and the traditional Evangelical services belong to the middle and higher strata of the upper classes). In terms of social classes, the lower strata of the middle class (80 per cent to 85 per cent) less skilled industrial workers and rural workers (15 per cent to 20 per cent) are predominant in Pentecostalism. When these lower strata of the population are drawn into Pentecostalism, they become subject to the influence of Pentecostal ideology, which is basically supported by two very cherished principles of Pentecostalism: belief in the power of the Spirit and obedience to the established authority, both derived from the Bible. The first principle is ahistorical and through it Pentecostals enter further into the sacral world, and it draws forth and brings into play the spontaneity and emotion usually present in popular religiosity. This belief in the power of God leads believers to see the evils of this world as signs of the coming of Christ, thus producing a misrepresentation of social reality. The second principle, however, is historical, and leads believers to passive submission to the established order, since it requires submissive and unquestioning behaviour towards the politico-social order. In this sense, Pentecostal religious ideology works culturally to condition people to continue capitalism in its present stage. It prevents the development of a capacity for critical reflection and submits believers to the dominant bourgeois ideology.

Meanwhile the Catholic Church has recently been awakening more and more to the mass aspirations of the people and towards its capacity to act reflectively. This is due to the development of the Church Basic Communities (*Communidades Eclesias de Base*). They are more and more numerous, and are to be found amongst the poorest social classes, working in urban and rural areas. The pedagogy in these communities seeks to integrate popular religious experience with a critical reflection about social realities. Popular religiousness moves forward hand in hand with a gradual awakening of the consciousness of the poor. This becomes evident in various ways, in terms either of material improvements in the neighbourhood or of taking on a considerable political dimension. As far as the social composition of these basic communities is concerned, we can say, on the basis of some local studies, that the lower strata of the middle class are predominant, together with working classes, albeit on a lesser scale. The basic communities can be distinguished clearly from the Pentecostal groups, not only because they are generally (but not exclusively) made up of Catholics, but also because religiousness goes hand in hand with critical reflection and social activity, which gradually permeates the different levels of society. In spite of the ambiguities, religion becomes aware by degrees of the specific contradictions of capitalist Brazilian society.

4. THE MESSAGE OF THE POOR

The poor and deprived experience all manner of things: democratic participation, popular politics, manipulation by popular leaders, religious proselytism and banishment for politico-social reasons. In spite of advances and reverses, their deliberative capacity is not yet dead. They bring a message in their own language and attitude. It is not the message that they are poor. It is, rather, mainly the message that they can repudiate their institutionalised situation of poverty and can state their capacity to realise possible alternatives of social organisation. This conscious repudiation of poverty which is not tied to the basic contradictions of dependent capitalism but does arise out of the midst of it tends to become consolidated as a form of protest against a structural situation and as a positive affirmation of its presence. The great majority of Pentecostal churches have shown themselves incapable of coping with the progressive awakening of this consciousness. The Catholic Church tries to cope with it through the basic communities. What matters, however, it that the 'option in favour of the poor' means that one meets them not as someone who has something to give but rather as someone who receives from them the inspired revelation about the direction in which this Church is to travel.

Translated by Isabel Ribeiro

Notes

1. Gino Germani 'Democracia representativa y classes populares' *Populismo y contradiciones de classes en Latinoamérica* (Mexico 1973) p. 21.
2. The basic communities (communidades de base) have become aware of this: 'The studies undertaken by priests does not help them to understand the people.' Dom Fragoso, addressing himself to the CEB in preparation for the inter-regional meeting in João Pessoa, said: 'In each state, the meeting will not be conducted by us priests, but by you farmers.'
3. See F. Rolim 'Aspects de la pratique dominicale au Brésil' *Social Compass* 14 No. 5–6 (1967).
4. See Emilio Willems 'El Protestantismo y los cambios culturales en Brasil y Chile' in *Revolucion, Religion y Reforma* (Barcelona 1969); Beatriz M. de Souza *A experiencia de salvação* (ed. Duas Cicadas 1969); Candido P. F. Camargo *Católicos, Protestantes e Espíritas* (ed. Vozes 1973).
5. Francisco C. Rolim *Pentecostalismo : Genese, estrutura e funções* (mimeographed 1973).

John Simpson

Work, Church Attendance and Happiness in the United States: An Empirical Analysis

WHILE many would argue that earthly happiness is neither the final goal nor the true measure of the life of man, it is difficult to deny its importance in human affairs. What is happiness and what are its sources? In this chapter I eschew the many and varied theological and philosophical answers that have been given to those questions (while not, of course, denying their importance) and focus upon whether men report that they are happy or unhappy when questioned. In particular, I will analyse the effects of the stratification of work and associated differences in the material conditions of life upon the self-reported happiness of individuals using data gathered from samples of respondents in the United States. At the same time, the effect of church attendance or what might be called 'conventional religiosity' upon happiness will also be assessed.

Subject to the limitations that are inherent in survey data and the methodology employed, the analysis provides an answer to the following question: Does religiosity, by affecting happiness, tend to offset or compensate for the poorer material conditions of those who occupy low positions in the structure of work? Both Marxist and non-Marxist social theorists have claimed that religion does have a compensatory effect among poorer people in industrial societies. The analysis in this chapter provides some empirical insight into that claim.

1. DATA AND METHODOLOGY

The data analysed in this chapter are taken from the General Social Survey (GSS) administered by the National Opinion Research Center of the University of Chicago. GSS data are gathered from national probability samples of the non-institutionalised population of the United States by interviewers using questionnaires. In terms of the usual standards applied to sample survey research data, GSS data are of very high quality since, for all practical purposes, they are free of sampling and non-response biases. From the combined GSS data sets for the years 1972 to 1977, the responses of employed males have been selected for analysis in this chapter.

Table 1 contains a cross-classification of respondents' replies to five questionnaire items: amount of education, occupation, income, frequency of church attendance, and degree of happiness. A respondent's position in the stratification of work is measured by the white collar/blue collar distinction. Differences in the material conditions of life are assumed to be reflected in the income variable and frequency of church attendance is used to measure 'conventional religiosity'. It should be noted that the church attendance item is a measure of a respondent's frequency of attendance at religious services without regard for the respondent's religious tradition or denominational affiliation. Education is included in *Table 1* because it is the single most important social factor in the United States affecting an individual's position in the stratification

Table 1

*Cross-Classification of Five Dichotomous Variables Measured in a Sample of Employed Males in the United States: A–Education, B–Occupation, C–Income, D–Church Attendance, E–Happiness**

A–Education[1]	*B–Occupation*	*C–Income*[2]	*D–Church Attendance*[3]	*E–Happiness*	
				High	*Low*
Low	White Collar	Low	Infrequent	31	82
High	White Collar	Low	Infrequent	25	58
Low	Blue Collar	Low	Infrequent	145	536
High	Blue Collar	Low	Infrequent	5	28
Low	White Collar	High	Infrequent	43	102
High	White Collar	High	Infrequent	71	101
Low	Blue Collar	High	Infrequent	104	218
High	Blue Collar	High	Infrequent	9	19
Low	White Collar	Low	Frequent	34	42
High	White Collar	Low	Frequent	23	42
Low	Blue Collar	Low	Frequent	102	213
High	Blue Collar	Low	Frequent	7	13
Low	White Collar	High	Frequent	38	45
High	White Collar	High	Frequent	46	84
Low	Blue Collar	High	Frequent	85	83
High	Blue Collar	High	Frequent	8	3

* Data are from the General Social Survey (GSS) for the years 1972 to 1977.
[1] Low = high school or less; High = more than high school.
[2] Low = $14,999 or less; High = more than $14,999. Figures are total family income.
[3] Infrequent = once a month or less; Frequent = more than once a month.

of work and, hence, his income. Happiness is the fifth and final variable in *Table 1*. While the subjective meaning of happiness may vary widely among individuals, the measure of happiness used in the GSS has been shown to be a reliable indicator of psychological well-being.

In the analysis of the data in *Table 1*, happiness is treated as a dependent variable that may be affected by education, occupation, income, church attendance or any combination of those variables. The method used to analyse the data results in an exact and exhaustive determination of those variables and combinations of variables that do and do not affect happiness. The details of the method are beyond the scope of this paper.[1] It is sufficient to note that the method has been shown to be defensible and fully satisfactory on mathematical and statistical grounds. That means, among other things, that the results obtained using the method are not an artifact of the method, itself, but are, rather, a valid indication of the structure of the data to which the method is applied.

2. FINDINGS

Table 2 contains the results of the analysis. As can be seen, income (C) and church attendance (D) have significant effects upon happiness. Furthermore, occupation and church attendance combine (BD) to effect happiness as do education, occupation and church attendance (ABD). Among the variables and combinations of variables that do not affect happiness, the insignificant impact of education (A), occupation (B) and the income-church attendance (CD) interaction deserve special attention and will be discussed below.

Table 2

Variables and Combinations of Variables that:

*Significantly Affect Happiness**	*Do Not Significantly Affect Happiness**
C, D	A, B
BD	AB, AC, BC, AD, CD
ABD	ABC, ACD, BCD
	ABCD

* Letters refer to the variables in *Table 1*.

In addition to the existence of the effects as reported in *Table 2*, the method employed to analyse the data in *Table 1* provides information about the direction and strength of those effects. The direction of the significant effects is as follows: a high degree of happiness is associated with high income (C), frequent church attendance (D), and being white collar and attending church frequently *or* with being blue collar and attending church infrequently (BD). The direction of the remaining significant effect (ABD) indicates, among other things, that respondents with high education who are white collar and attend church infrequently *and* those with low education who are blue collar and attend church frequently are likely to report a high rather than a low degree of happiness.

Of the four significant effects upon happiness reported in *Table 2*, the frequency of church attendance (D) has the strongest impact. The magnitudes of the other significant effects upon happiness, each as a percentage of the magnitude of the effect of church attendance, are as follows: income (C), 67 per cent; occupation and church attendance (BD), 50 per cent; education, occupation, and church attendance (ABD), 57 per cent.

3. DISCUSSION

Perhaps, the moststriking finding is the powerful positive effect that church attendance has upon happiness. As noted, income has only two-thirds of the impact that church attendance hasupon happiness. Thus, in one of the most advanced capitalist societies in the world, today, where the individual is constantly bombarded by the media with the message that to consume is to be happy, the practice of religion has a more powerful impact upon an individual's happiness than does the possession of the means of consumption, namely, income. Furthermore, neither the structure of work (the white collar/blue collar distinction) nor education contribute directly to happiness although an extension of the analysis would, undoubtedly, show that both affect happiness indirectly through their effects upon income since white collar workers and the highly educated have higher incomes than blue collar workers and the less well educated. Conventional religiosity, then, as measured by church attendance, stands alongside the education-occupation-income complex as an independent and powerful determinate of self-reported happiness in the United States.

I turn now to the question of whether church attendance interacts with income to affect happiness. Do individuals who have low incomes and attend church frequently report a significantly high degree of happiness? If they do, then support would exist for the proposition that religiosity tends to offset or compensate for the negative effect of low income upon happiness. In fact, the data in *Table 1* do not support that proposition since the income-church attendance combination (CD), as reported in *Table 2*, is not significant. There is, therefore, no suggestion in the data under examination that frequent church attendance compensates for low income by increasing an individual's happiness. To the extent, then, that the data and methodology provide a test of the popular sociological notion that religion has a compensatory affect among poorer people, the notion is rejected.

While religiosity in the United States appears to have no compensatory effect among poorer people, the significant BD (occupation and church attendance) and ABD (education, occupation, and church attendance) interactions suggest that religiosity combines with education and occupation as prestige factors to affect happiness (apart from income). The BD combination may, perhaps, indicate that church attendance tends to be the norm in white collar culture while infrequent church attendance is the expectation among blue collar workers. The significant ABD combination suggests that, among white collar workers, high education is an alternative to frequent church attendance as a resource for securing happiness while, among blue collar workers, low levels of education are offset by frequent church attendance. Thus, although the results of the analysis do not support the proposition that religiosity compensates the poor by increasing their happiness, they do suggest that religiosity interacts in complex ways with status attributes such as occupation and education and to affect happiness.

In conclusion I make three observations. First, the fact that in a sample of the population of the United States religiosity does not have a compensatory effect among the less-well-to-do undoubtedly would not be observed in many other populations, especially those in the Third World nations. There religiosity and various kinds of ideological commitments may dramatically temper the harshness of the material conditions of life. Such, indeed, may even be the case among the very poor in the United States who, because of their relatively small numbers, would have little impact upon the findings derived from sample survey data like that analysed in this chapter.

The finding of no compensatory effect in the data does suggest an interesting proposition worth some thought: Relative prosperity may be a condition for the existence and practice of humanising, non-alienating religion; the lower the absolute amount of wealth in a collectivity and the more unequal the distribution of wealth, the more likely religion will be, on the one hand, an opiate for the poor and, on the other hand, an ideological justification for the rich.

Second, it was found that *both* the material conditions of life which flow from an individual's position in the structure of work and religiosity affect happiness or well-being. While the effect of religiosity upon happiness is larger than the effect of income, both have a significant impact. That being the case, it would seem to follow that philosophical and theological considerations of well-being and the human condition must take into account both the material and the spiritual conditions of life. They cannot be divorced. Consideration of one aspect entails consideration of the other.

Finally, I note that happiness or individual well-being is, itself, an ambiguous state or condition in terms of its consequences. On the one hand, the individual who is happy or in a state of well-being may, himself, contribute to the personal well-being and joy of others. On the other hand, however, the happy individual may be so self-satisfied and self-possessed that he is blind to the needs of others and to the forces of evil and domination at work in the world. To the extent that happiness has ambiguous consequences, the determinates of happiness—religiosity and the material resources that flow from the structure of work—are, themselves, enveloped in ambiguity. Both work and religiosity, then, contribute to the joy and to the misery of human life. That mystery is only resolved, ultimately, in the divine economy.

Notes

1. See L. A. Goodman 'A Modified Multiple Regression Approach to the Analysis of Dichotomous Variables' *American Sociological Review* 37 (1972) 28.

Władysław Piwowarski

Continuity and Change in Polish Popular Religion

INTRODUCTION

POLISH popular religion is a subject on which there are many views, both in Poland itself and abroad. These views are being expressed particularly frequently at present as a result of the election of a Pole as pope. In Poland many people believe that the election of John Paul II was brought about by the Polish Catholic Church's achievement in successfully resisting the process of laicisation both among individuals and in the national life and retaining its vitality in spite of unfavourable conditions in the shape of the socialist system and the spread of atheist ideology. With such a diversity of views it is worth while examining the appearance Polish religion presents in sociological terms, to see which elements are relatively stable, which are undergoing change, and what tendencies these changes represent. This article will deal with these problems, not just generally, but also with reference to specific social categories.

It should be said that studies of religious attitudes in Polish society have been carried out now for more than twenty years. In spite of the growing tendencies to adopt 'ideological' frameworks, both among Catholic and among marxist sociologists, the main emphasis has continued to be on empirical studies based on the theoretical and methodological foundations accepted by practitioners of social science throughout the world. However, most of these studies were limited in scope and it is therefore difficult to make useful generalisations. Here we shall do no more than set out various hypotheses which require verification by further studies in the sociology of religion.[1]

There is an established model for the analysis of Polish popular religion which was developed by Polish sociologists and students of culture soon after the first world war and has been largely verified and accepted by modern Polish sociology of religion.[2] This model contains the following elements: (*a*) a deep and emotional attachment to the faith, but with a predominance of cultural motivations; (*b*) a defective intellectual appropriation or even plain religious ignorance; (*c*) ritualism in religious views and behaviour patterns; (*d*) a relatively high degree of acceptance of religious dogmas and a markedly lower degree of acceptance of moral principles; (*e*) a weak association between religion and morality, especially in the case of social morality; (*f*) a relatively strong identification with religious institutions, especially the parish or local community; (*g*) attachment to religious leaders, especially when they are authentic leaders. The model of Polish popular religion has connections with the culturally and environmentally conditioned type of religion, that is, this sort of religion relies more on the 'tradition of the fathers' than on the personal decision of Catholics.

1. FACTORS OF CONTINUITY AND CHANGE

Polish popular religion has been able to survive as a traditional religion with all the negative and positive features of that type as a result of the complex action of four factors on a relatively high level. These are the following.

(*a*) The continuation of religious life in the familial environment. The transmission of traditional cultural patterns of behaviour, including patterns of religious behaviour, depends largely on the type and character of the family. Particularly privileged in this respect is the family group consisting of three generations in direct sequence. Sociologists have pointed out the phenomenon of the social continuity or reproduction of cultural attitudes through the generations, and it has even been said that the family passes on religious life as an 'inheritance'.[3] As in other industrialised countries, this type of family group is rapidly disappearing, especially in the cities, but a model which is retained is that of the 'extended family', in which the grandparents look after the children at least temporarily. In addition there is a tendency in the families to maintain social contacts with relatives, irrespective of where they live. All this encourages cultural, social and religious continuity.

(*b*) The connection between Catholicism and the Polish national tradition. For centuries Catholicism in Poland has had an important integrating function and has been a symbol of national identification and independence. An important element in this were religious practices involving mass participation. Participation in religious practices and rites was proof of membership, not merely of the Catholic Church, but also of the Polish nation, though not of the State or higher social classes. This ambiguity of affiliation has survived into the present. After the second world war an element of opposition was added because of the Church's role as the only real force in Polish society apart from the socialist state.

(*c*) Mass pastoral care. The activities of the Polish Church are directed to the mass of Catholics, or the 'average Catholic'. This can be seen not only in pastoral programmes and activities, but also in the forms and methods of pastoral work. The result of such work is the maintenance of the model of traditional religion, and of the ambiguity as between membership of Church and State, and the overall aim is, as one is told, to keep the mass of Catholics in the Church.

(*d*) The socialist system. The symbiosis between the Church and the ruling classes was in the past a source of anti-clericalism. The separation of Church and State after the second world war eliminated such sources, and even produced increased sympathy for the Church. Moreover, socialism, as a system based on Marxist ideology, seeks to produce an atheist society; consequently, it has frequently met opposition in cultural matters, and traditional values such as God and religion have always been part of the stock of the national culture. Any attempt to eliminate them therefore provoked opposition. Socialism starts from the premise of theoretical materialism, but does not encourage practical materialism, which seems to be one of the roots of the crisis of religious practice in highly developed countries.

The combination of factors mentioned here encourages the maintenance of the model of traditional religion, but this does not mean that there are not also other factors which produce changes in at least some elements of this model. These changes seem to be determined by two fundamental processes, induced and spontaneous laicisation.

'Induced laicisation' means, negatively, 'the task of eliminating the influences and control of religion and religious organisations and the cleansing of the "profane sphere" from "the sacral"', but positively the emergence of new structures which 'no longer take their direction from religion', such as world-views, ideologies and culture. Laicisation understood in this way contains 'implicitly a specific ideology, based on the principles of Marxist philosophy'.[4] In other words, the process of induced laicisation is directed towards the abolition of religious alienation, towards the propagation of atheism. It includes both the consciousness of human individuals and public life. In Poland its results, in spite of a heavy concentration on religion, are hard to determine because of a double opposition. On the one hand, there is that of the 'traditional forces' of Polish society, and on the other institutional opposition, connected with the activity of the Catholic Church. The Catholic Church in Poland exaggerates to some extent when it assesses the process of induced laicisation while at the same time underestimating the results of the process of spontaneous laicisation.

The process of spontaneous laicisation covers the emancipation of various areas of society such as politics, science, philosophy, culture, education and training, leisure, etc. from domination by Church institutions and religious systems of meaning.[5] In a more radical understanding, spontaneous laicisation is a process in which religious attitudes, practices and institutions lose their social significance. It is well known that this process takes place with particular intensity wherever two other processes, industrialisation and urbanisation, have become established.[6] In Poland the results of spontaneous laicisation, in spite of intensive (so-called 'socialist') industrialisation and urbanisation, are less marked than elsewhere, and this is due to the particular character of Polish religion and its unique features. Nevertheless sociologists of religion have noted certain changes in the model of religion described above, which is no longer universally valid and also no longer the only model. We may add that Marxist sociologists, because of their doctrinal principles, see only one direction of change, from popular religion to the absence of religion and atheism. Catholic sociologists take a significantly broader view of these changes and their significance, especially in the scientific centres. We must now ask, therefore, what elements of Polish popular religion are remaining stable and what are changing.

2. ELEMENTS OF CONTINUITY AND CHANGE

When one considers the features of Polish popular religion we have listed, it must be borne in mind that a deep emotional attachment to the faith exists today, just as in the past. The sociological survey carried out nationally in 1960 produced the following results:[7]

	Village	*Town*
Committed believers	26·1%	19·4%
Believers	57·7%	56·2%
Really unbelievers but having links with the tradition	8·3%	12·1%
Indifferent	6·3%	9·2%
Unbelievers	1·1%	3·1%
No answer	0·5%	—

As the table shows, the overall proportion of committed and other believers totalled at the time 83·8 per cent in the country and 75·6 per cent in the towns. This situation has hardly changed in the intervening years. A similar survey carried out in 1977 showed that in Poland 88·9 per cent of the population regarded themselves as Catholics, 1·0 per cent as members of other religious groups, and 8·4 per cent as unconnected with any religious group or sect. The proportion of refusals to answer was 1·7 per cent.[8] Considered from a different point of view, the figure for committed Catholics was 18·0 per cent, for believers 68·4 per cent, for the indifferent 5·7 per cent, for complete unbelievers 6·4 per cent and for refusals to answer 1·5 per cent. These surveys showed that the overall proportion of the committed and otherwise religious population was 86·4 per cent, with no major changes in the figures for villages and towns. A feature of the results is that while there has been a slight decline in the category of committed believers, the number of believers has risen, though the increase is minimal. Generally, we can say that, in spite of the effects of the processes of laicisation, both induced and spontaneous, the overall figure for the proportion of the Polish population who are believers and connected with the Catholic Church remains high. After the visit of Pope John Paul II to Poland the number of believers probably increased.

The more detailed studies examined the reasons for belief. Widespread reasons for belief among the rural and urban population of Poland are the influence of the family, and education, the influence of popular and national traditions and the influence of the local environment. Reasons showing evidence of convictions or personal decision appeal much less frequently. It is nevertheless typical that of the two parameters of the tradition, the temporal and the spatial, the first is much more frequently emphasised than the second. This means that religion in Poland is firmly rooted in family, regional and national tradition. Asked why they were believers, most people replied: 'Because our fathers and forefathers were also believers.'

Despite the high percentage of believers, the sociological surveys produced low figures for knowledge of religion. In this respect there is no difference between town and country. Only 40 per cent of the population have what would be in the eyes of the Catholic Church a relatively adequate knowledge of religion. The rest show inadequate or simply defective knowledge. Deepening intellectual appreciation of the faith is a real problem in Poland. As a result, the pastoral campaigns undertaken by the bishops are inadequate and contribute more to preserving traditional religion than to developing it.

The main feature of Polish Catholicism is the ritualism shown in views and practices. In views, the majority of Polish Catholics regard ritual duties, i.e., the performance of religious practices, as their main duties. And they do take part in these practices. The 1960 survey produced the following results:[9]

	Village	*Town*
practising regularly	46·7%	35·6%
practising irregularly	33·3%	34·0%
rarely practising	12·8%	17·9%
non-practising	6·3%	12·3%
no answer	0·9%	0·2%

The total figure for practising Catholics (irregular and regular) was then 80 per cent in the country and 69·6 per cent in the towns. The two categories include Catholics who went to mass at least once a month. In 1977 the situation was the following:[10]

practising regularly	48·3%
practising irregularly	21·4%
rarely practising	19·0%
non-practising	10·3%
no answer	1·1%

The total percentage of practising Catholics (regular and irregular) was 69·7 per cent. There were no comparative data for town and country. The level of religious practice has remained high—indeed, the figure for practising Catholics as risen steadily [*sic*].

Another feature of Polish religion is the attitude of Catholics to religious truths and moral principles. In the past their acceptance of these was based on trust in the authority of the Church and tradition. Now there are signs that this type of legitimation is disappearing—a situation connected with the process of rationalisation and increasing critical distance from the Church. Accordingly, Polish Catholics are beginning to deny particular religious truths or doubt them. This phenomenon is commoner in towns and industrial areas than in the traditional villages. As an example we cite data from three industrial towns, Nowa Huta, Płock and Pułway. Sociological surveys were carried out in 1970 in these three towns with a representative sample of the population. In order, the acceptance of religious truths in the three towns looks like this:[11]

divinity of Christ:	84·9%	81·8%	81·2%
eternal life:	70·9%	56·7%	69·8%
resurrection at the last judgement:	57·8%	44·5%	50·5%
sacrament of forgiveness of sins:	67·8%	54·8%	65·4%

Even greater differences, and still lower figures, were recorded for acceptance of moral principles.

The weak side of Polish religion has been the connection between religion and moral life, especially social morality. This can still be seen today, in spite of the high figures for belief and practice. In Poland the influence of religion on habits is slight, for example in the areas of marriage, work, respect for public property, the cultivation of sobriety, the keeping of feast-days and resistance to apathy. Ritual norms are still more important in Polish religion than the evangelical ideals. Nevertheless there is currently a growing number of Catholics who are emphasising the 'consequences' of religion; this has been shown by a number of studies.[12]

A further feature of Polish religion is identification with the parish or local community. In the past the parish was an important integrating force, performing both religious and non-religious functions. Industrialisation and urbanisation are leading to the break-up of the local community, to the 'atomisation' of the parish, with a resulting decline in the number of Catholics who identify with the parish. In the towns previously mentioned (Nowa Huta, Płock and Puławy), 4·5 per cent, 5·6 per cent and 10 per cent identify fully with the parish, 40 per cent, 21 per cent and 16·1 per cent do not identify at all with the parish, and there is an intermediate group of 'users' or 'sympathisers' of the parish.[13] An interesting development, however, is the spread of religious groups including both young people and adults, based on a structure of small groups. Two of these are particularly important, the *Neokatechumenat* and *Oaza* (*'Światło i Życie'*, 'Light and Life'). The first group contains about 5 000 adults, and the second about 40 000 young people. Their influence on communal religious life is significant, especially where religious organisations are banned.

The final feature of Polish religion we shall discuss is attachment to religious leaders. The priest has always been seen as the most important link between the believer or the community and the sacred. In many surveys the question 'Is the mediation of a priest necessary for salvation?' was answered affirmatively by over 90 per cent of respondents.[14] It is widely held in Poland that the preservation and development of Polish religion depends overwhelmingly on the personal characteristics and behaviour of the priest. The priest certainly enjoys high prestige in society, and that may be one of the reasons for the large number of vocations. Because of the inadequacies of the administrative system, the role of the priest in the past was given a very broad definition. The clergy were leaders in many areas of life. Today their importance is gradually declining, but their influence is still greater than in many countries. On the other hand, the Polish clergy has not escaped the crisis; this can be seen most clearly in the type of personal pastoral work and in the growing need for more direct contacts.

This very general outline of the features of Polish religion illustrates not just the general features of this religion, which is that of the whole society, but also its strengths and weaknesses. And these strengths and weaknesses are being revealed more clearly than before by present cultural and social changes. One result of these changes is a decrease in the significance of those who, on this model, may be called traditional Catholics, while at the same time new models or, better, movements for change are appearing which are marked by a degree of pluralism. In general there are two main tendencies in Poland, on the one hand an effort to loosen or dismantle the ties of tradition and on the other efforts to deepen religious life. Of these two broad tendencies the first is more widespread than the second. In an intermediate position is the tendency for a selective religion to spread; this is the dominant tendency. The changes in religious life in Poland are similar to those in other advanced countries, but are taking place more slowly because of the particular features described above.

In general, atheism in Polish society has only a marginal influence on these changes. Much more widespread is religious indifference, though that too is not the main tendency. Both lines of change, however, lead to the abandonment of the model of traditional religion with the result that individuals do not construct any world-view of their own. This situation can be found even among enlightened atheists. In people affected by this tendency there is often some 'residual religion', expressed in private practices and the observance of some religious traditions. The tendency to deepen religious life is also not very widespread in Polish society, though it is significant because it is based on the experience of religion as a personal value, leads to commitment in religious communities and makes a connection between religion and moral life. Catholics of this sort no longer draw their inspiration just from traditional religion, but also from the post-conciliar Church. The most widespread tendency, finally, as already mentioned, is that towards selectivity in religion. It is shown by a merely partial identification with the faith and the Church. Those affected by it regard themselves as believers, and in some sense also as practising, but do not fully share either the doctrines of the Church (dogmas of faith and moral principles), nor do they take an active part in community life. Selectivity appears in all the fundamental measures of religious life in which choice and commitment are involved.[15]

The development of a selective attitude towards religion is much less the result of atheistic propaganda than of membership of an industrial culture. This new social form of religion has not yet developed distinctly and appears disparate. Probably it is a form of religion not requiring any decision of substance,[16] or an extra-institutional, private religion.[17]

The changes indicated can be explained by schemata which are familiar in their main lines, that of 'subject-object agreement'[18] or that of 'affect-knowledge dissonance'.[19] Polish sociologists also have more specific theories of change which draw attention to particular features and factors which differentiate and influence the religious life of Catholics. These can for the most part be divided into three groups: (*a*) demographic features, (*b*) social features, and (*c*) social factors.

There are two important demographic features, age and sex structure. Many specialised studies argue that the level of religious activity is dependent on age and sex, with a greater intensity among men than women. As regards the age structure, it is clear that the curve of religious activity reaches its highest point in children and young people, falls in people between the ages of twenty-five and forty-five, and finally rises again in old people, though the initial level is never reached again. This statement applies particularly to religious practices. In the case of other parameters of religious activity the age-related situation is more complex. It has been noted in Poland, for example, that the younger generation, especially young people during their education, practise more than their elders, but believe less, measured in terms of acceptance of religious dogmas and moral principles.

There are also two main social features, educational structure and occupational structure. Educational structure seems to have an important influence on the level of religious activity, which can be summed up as: The higher the level of education the lower the level of religious activity. The relation between occupational structure and religious activity is much less clear, though people in occupations which have lower social status and demand less skill show a higher level of religious activity.

Among the social factors examined were the size of the housing development, the effect of industrialisation and urbanisation, and the migration of the rural population to the towns. As regards the first factor, it is striking that the larger the social environment is, and the more open to the influences of civilisation, the lower is the level of religious activity. Nevertheless, the influence of industrialisation and urbanisation on religion is not always clearly negative; the influences of traditional forces and of the Church in particular may be moderating influences. Lastly, with regard to migration it seems that in the first phase of village people's contact with the town the level of religious activity falls. Later, however, as they become used to the urban environment, there is a revival and stabilisation of religious life. This is more likely where the people have come to the town from relatively near than where they come from farther away.

The variables listed here as influencing religious activity have the character of 'partial variables', with the exception of the level of education, which, under Polish conditions, has the character of a 'global variable' and mediates other variables. It has been found that a rise in the level of education leads on the one hand to increased involvement in industrial culture and on the other to greater criticism of the cultural tradition. In religion this appears mainly as a search for an independent basis, selectivity in attitudes and behaviour and criticism of the Church. Nevertheless sympathy for religion as a part of the national heritage remains. The second 'global variable', and one which is given too little attention in sociological analyses, is the history and tradition of the region. Silesia is particularly interesting, since here, in spite of intensive industrialisation, the level of religious activity is very high.

CONCLUSION

The aim of this description of Polish popular religion has been to indicate, at least in broad outline, its continuity under the conditions resulting from a society which is building socialism, that is, under the conditions produced by a system which totally excludes religion. At the same time we have tried to illustrate the changes in progress as a result of induced and spontaneous laicisation. Some features of this religion, with traditional roots in Polish national culture, are able to survive despite the changes taking place in society and culture; these include attachment to the faith of the fathers, participation in religious practices, especially those with a mass character, and devotion to religious leaders in a blend of religion and nationalism. It should be added that among the features persisting unchanged are some which should have been changed by pastoral action, such as ignorance in religion, ritualism, the absence of conscious personal motivation and the weak connection between religion and morality. Nevertheless, in spite of the continuity of Polish popular religion, it is undergoing changes, affecting both religious attitudes and religious behaviour. The principal signs of these are doubt or denial of religious dogmas and moral principles and the loosening of ties with the local church as a result of reduced participation in its activities, which is a sign of increasing critical distance from the Church. One result of these changes is selectivity in attitude and involvement in the life of the Church. These changes in religious activity seem to have been due more to the development of modern civilisation than to the propaganda of the Marxist-Leninist party. It therefore seems reasonable to suppose that the further development of these changes will resemble that in the advanced countries of Western Europe. The particular character of Polish conditions does no more than slow down and modify the process. It is hard to predict how long the existing situation can continue, or what the future of Polish religious life will be, if pastoral work continues to follow the lines of the last thirty years.

Translated from the German by Francis McDonagh

Notes

1. The nature of the surveys carried out into Polish religion has been described in more detail in the collective work edited by W. Piwowarski *Religijność polska—Studia z sociologii religii* (Warsaw [in press]).
2. See S. Czarnowski 'Kultura religijna wieskiego ludu polskiego' in *Dzieła* (Works) (Warsaw 1956) I pp. 88-107.
3. See F. Boulard, J. Rémy *Pratique religieuse urbaine et religions culturelles* (Paris 1968) p. 122; L. Voyé *Sociologie du geste religieux* (Brussels 1973) pp. 220-221.
4. J. F. Godlewski *Kościół rzymsko-katolicki w Polsce wobec sekularysacji życia publicznego* (Warsaw 1978) pp. 14-15.
5. See P. Berger and T. Luckmann 'Secularisation and Pluralism' *Internationales Jahrbuch für Religionssoziologie* (Cologne and Opladen 1966) II p. 74.
6. B. Wilson 'The Debate over "Secularisation": Religion, Society, Faith' *Encounter* 45 (1975) 79.
7. A. Pawełczyńska 'Postawy ludnośći wiejskiej wobec religii' *Roczniki Sociologii Wsi. Studia i Materialy* (Yearbook of Village Sociology, Studies and Materials) (Warsaw 1970) VIII p. 73.
8. Information from a paper read in the P.T.S.
9. Pawełczyńska, in the article cited in note 7, at p. 74.
10. See note 8.
11. See W. Piwowarski *Religijność miejska w rejonie uprzemysłowionym* (Warsaw 1977) pp. 195-201.
12. More detailed surveys of religious attitudes are being carried out by the Department of the Sociology of Religion at the Catholic University of Lublin, but the results have for the most part not yet been published.
13. Piwowarski, in the book cited in note 1 at pp. 295-313.
14. *Ibid.* pp. 319-325.
15. See J. Mariański 'Dynamika przemian religijności wiejskiej w warunkach industrializacji' *Chrześcijanin w świecie* (Christian in the World) 11 No. 4 (1979) 62-66.
16. See H. O. Wölber *Religion ohne Entscheidung* (Göttingen 1956) p. 51.
17. See P. M. Zulehner *Religion nach Wahl. Grundlegung einer Auswahlchristenpastoral* (Vienna 1974) pp. 13-50.
18. See E. Pin *Pratique religieuse et classes sociales dans une paroisse urbaine: Saint-Pothin à Lyon* (Paris 1956) pp. 263-264.
19. See G. Schmidtchen *Zwischen Kirche und Gesellschaft. Forschungsbericht über die Umfragen zur Gemeinsamen Synode der Bistümer in der B.R.D.* (Freiburg im Breisgau 1972) pp. 40 ff.
20. Sociological surveys have twice been repeated after ten years in Poland, in the village region of Płock in 1978 (J. Mariański) and in the urban area of Pułway in 1979 (W. Piwowarski).

Srdjan Vrcan

Social Class and Religion in Yugoslavia

IT IS generally recognised that Yugoslav society as a whole, inclusive of the religious elements in it, is a social reality of such unusual complexity that there are few parallels anywhere in Europe. The population of contemporary Yugoslavia belonged for centuries to different political and religious worlds. Within the limits of the same country there are at least six major national and ethnic groups of Slavic origin living side by side, frequently intermingled, and also several non-Slavic ethnic groups, including for instance an Albanian community living in a compact region that has become larger in size than some national groups of Slavic origin. The dominant religions are Roman Catholic, Orthodox, and Islamic, each linked to cultural and national identifications that have histories of age-old conflicts, the remnants of which still exert certain pressures on Yugoslav society. All religions, moreover, have taken a hostile attitude toward the arrival of modern society, first in the brief bourgeois phase and later in the present socialist form. They were afraid that industrialisation would undermine the influence of religion upon the people; and they are strongly opposed to the radical secularism of official socialist culture. Yugoslavia is also special because its form of socialism includes moments of decentralisation and workers' participation, for which there are no parallels in Eastern Europe. These are some of the reasons why social scientific research dealing with Yugoslav society in general can come to conclusions only after extensive and detailed empirical inquiries, concentrating on the various nations, regions, ethnic communities and religious groups, each of which may present conditions that vary considerably due to the particular character of their histories. In this article, therefore, we shall limit ourselves to reflections on the empirical research that has been done on religion and social class in areas of the country that are predominantly Roman Catholic. From this research we hope to draw a few conclusions.

1. BEYOND IDEOLOGICAL PERSPECTIVES

It is sometimes assumed that the uniqueness and the apparently exceptional character of the contemporary situation lies exclusively in the fact that the dominant social system in Yugoslavia is a socialist one, relegating religion to the private sphere of life and promoting a secular official culture. On this assumption it is insisted in one specific ideological perspective that it is the spreading of secular culture with its totalising tendencies, the expansion of religious indifference and irreligion and a considerable disaffection from traditional religion in some social strata in Yugoslavia that are to be taken as problematic and in some sense unexpected, not natural and normal and consequently in need of an adequate theoretical explanation. At the same time the existence of religion and the persistence of religious culture with its own traditional totalising claims in contemporary Yugoslav society are considered to be essentially non-problematic, natural and normal, and consequently not demanding a specific theoretical explanation. In this case the explanatory scheme that comes to the fore is one that insists on the direct impact of the dominant social system, on the existence of institutional pressure, on social control, etc. The existing trend towards religious indifference and irreligion in contemporary Yugoslav society in general and in some specific social classes in that society is then to be explained in such general terms.

It is interesting that the same assumption appears in another ideological guise. For in another perspective it is assumed that the uniqueness of the Yugoslav situation makes the persistence, stability and vitality of religion in that society and in some specific social classes unexpected and highly problematic and in need of a plausible theoretical explanation. In this case the preferable explanatory scheme to be used is one that concentrates on the low educational and informational level, the cultural immaturity and social marginality of certain social strata. The persisting commitment to religion in general and its strength in particular social classes is to be theoretically accounted for primarily in such terms. These two ideological perspectives give rise to a paradox, namely, that the same or very similar phenomena and trends—either of persisting or of declining commitment to religion by some social classes in comparison to others in the same society—come to be explained in quite different theoretical terms depending on the nature of the dominant social system concerned, For instance, the relatively high incidence of declining commitment to religion and the expansion of religious indifference and irreligion in some social strata with high social status in contemporary Yugoslav society are reasonably accounted for in terms of the impact of the dominant socialist social system, institutional pressure and social control, the nature of the educational system, etc. But the relatively high incidence of expanding commitment to religion among the upper and middle classes in some other contemporary industrial society in Western Europe, i.e. Italy or France, is not to be accounted for in the same or similar terms. The same paradox reappears when it comes to account for the positive or negative correlations between the levels of commitment to religion and the levels of formal school education depending on the nature of dominant social systems concerned.

Consequently, in order to avoid such and similar paradoxes it seems reasonable to hypothesise, at the present-day level of systematic exploration of the problem, that there exists the same or very similar historical and social 'problematic background' common to the religious situation in contemporary Yugoslav society and in some Western European industrial societies. This common historical and social 'problematic background' may be described as the manifest tensions between religion and irreligion, commitment to religion and religious indifference, involvement in the church and the sharing of a secular cultural totalisation. It could be assumed that in spite of very important differences and peculiarities there are some identical or very similar structural trends in operation in such societies, even when expressed manifestly in apparently opposite forms and ways.

2. FOUR GENERAL CONCLUSIONS

The still only initial empirical investigations and more or less preliminary theoretical discussions of the problem of social classes and religion in contemporary Yugoslav society (at least referring to the parts of the country with dominant Christian and primarily Roman Catholic tradition and relatively higher level of industrialisation and urbanisation) have indicated the following conclusions.

1. First, the effective commitment to religion and involvement in the church in terms of internalising the existing religious symbols with their respective religious beliefs, values and norms is neither evenly nor randomly distributed in contemporary Yugoslav society (i.e. in a human population, making up a complex, structurally differentiated and conflict-ridden society), but depends, in some way empirically to be explored, upon the vitally important differences in general 'social position' and in total 'existential situation' of different sections of that population. These investigations and discussions tend to confirm rather than question the traditional sociological theoretical insight that some

vitally important social differences in purely secular aspects of social position and existential situation resulting in widely differing qualities of everyday life and of typical life chances, do, under certain circumstances, make a difference in the commitment to religion and do have some visible consequences on the involvement in church. And this is so, in spite of three relevant facts:

(*a*) First, the fact that the religion concerned may be addressed equally to all regardless of any difference in social position and existential situation. This religion may be operating with the universal claims, at the doctrinal and practical level, to be the necessary, permanent, central and normal ingredient to human life, defining unequivocally what is of ultimate and non-ultimate concern and what is to be considered moral, social, political and cultural normality; (*b*) secondly, the fact the religion concerned may have been present for centuries in the given area as the only valid and unchallenged cultural complex; (*c*) and thirdly, the fact that this is happening in a population that, contrary to some appearances and assumptions, has almost totally been in contact with religion and the church, at least on the elementary or conventional level, such as being baptised, having received first communion, having at least a minimal degree of catechetical instruction, etc.[1]

We note that the same conclusion, our first, could also be validated for the official culture and the symbolic system promoted and propagated by the social system. The official culture with its specific symbolism is not evenly or randomly distributed in the same population, it is being internalised in different ways by different sections of the population, even by those to whom it is directly and primarily addressed.

2. The second conclusion that comes out from the initial investigations and discussions of this problem is that the different social classes and in particular the 'great social classes' in the historical sense, to use Marx's own terms, including some intermediate social strata or middle classes, show different general attitudes to religion. They are heirs of differing historical and cultural facts and consequently tend to develop different levels of commitment to religion and involvement in church, at least in a manifest manner. Such different levels of attitudes and commitment by different social classes and strata seem to be of a systematic nature in contemporary Yugoslav society. It would be very hard to prove that they are casual phenomena or by-products of some accidental concurrence of historical, social and cultural circumstances. In fact, such differences reappear in different parts of the country, for instance in parts of Slovenia and Croatia, but obviously not always with the same intensity and magnitude. And they reappear in a systematic way if one takes into account different empirical indicators of possible commitment to religion and involvement in church, for instance religious affiliation, personal religi-

ous identification, religious practice, acknowledging traditional, doctrinally fixed religious beliefs, etc.

3. The third conclusion seems to be that the general attitude of the members of a social class or stratum to religion and church, although structurally articulated, is not an independent variable, but depends on some specific combination of historical, political and cultural circumstances. There seems to be some specific combination of conditions, primarily structured in terms of locality, region and nationality, that have an important impact on the commitment to religion and involvement in the church of the same social class and stratum in different localities and regions. This could be illustrated by data from a research of the working-class youth employed in the same type of industry (shipbuilding industry) but located in different regions along the Adriatic Coast. The self-identification of working-class youth respondents varied from 43·2 per cent identified as believers in Split to 20·8 per cent in Pula and 14·3 per cent in Rijeka.[2] The same difference, but at a lower level reappears in regular Sunday practice with 13·5 per cent of working-class youth respondents regularly practising in Split compared to 2·4 per cent in other shipyards. It may be reasonably assumed that commitment to religion depends in some way in contemporary Yugoslav society on so-called contextual variables (*variables contextuelles*, according to the terms used by G. Michelat and M. Simon), which is unrelated to the fact that Yugoslav society is socialist, with a radically secular official culture.

The same phenomenon has been observed by other sociologists in some other West-European societies with predominant Catholic religious background and a late capitalist social system. It seems probable that this depends on actually existing structural distinctions between different localities and regions within the same society, some highly urbanised and some predominantly of rural character retaining a traditional peasant civilisation. Localities and regions with predominantly rural traditions in general show relatively the highest levels of commitment to religion, regardless of class distinctions. But there is no linear correlation between the level of urbanisation and the level of average commitment to religion and involvement in the church. Some of the most urbanised regions are not necessarily the areas with the lowest average level of commitment to religion and involvement in the church. But it would be an unwarranted generalisation to conclude that this is essentially due to the appearance of a new religiosity of contemporary urban type. It may be due to the fact that in the contemporary urban population of Yugoslavia almost every third inhabitant of the cities has been born in a village and has moved to the city from a rural area. The rapid process of urbanisation seems to be accompanied by a kind of ruralisation of urban areas. There has been some expansion and intrusion of traditional rural ways of life and conduct into certain cities and urban areas. At the same time it is reasonable to presume that the local and regional differences in respect of the commitment to religion and involvement in the church go back far into history and are a consequence of a long historical process. There is some truth in the assertion of a sociologist of religion of Catholic orientation that the first inn in a village has been historically the first 'anti-church'.[3] In fact, history has recorded that there have always been some pious villages, towns and regions as well as some having the 'bad' reputation of being impious ones.

4. The fourth conclusion is that in spite of the empirically verified and verifiable differences in commitment to religion and involvement in church of different social classes and social strata, there is no social stratum of some numerical relevance that could be located beyond the existing tensions between religion and irreligion, commitment to religion and lack of such commitment, integration in religious cultural totalisation and integration in secular cultural totalisation, etc. In fact this tension seems to be felt in all social classes and in all social strata of some numerical relevance. Therefore, there are no religiously totally homogeneous social classes and strata from peasantry to intelligentsia. The distinction between individuals commmitted to religion and the religiously non-committed appears in all social classes of some numerical relevance, but in different magnitudes. It is only the traditional peasantry that comes closest to being an exception by showing a very high degree of religious homogeneity. On the other side, it is only some restricted section of the upper social strata with highest social status as defined by official culture that comes closest to being an exception in the opposite sense by showing a high degree of irreligion. But this is probably not anything peculiar to contemporary Yugoslav society. The same phenomenon exists in some other European societies with a different social system.

A general conclusion seems to be warranted: Neither the persisting religious cultural totalisation as measured by commitment to religion and involvement in the church, nor the existing secular cultural totalisation sustained by the social system have created culturally and symbolically impenetrable barriers to isolate and culturally encapsulate in a total way any section of the population. The commitment to religion as well as the lack of such commitment remain a majority/minority affair in almost all numerically relevant sections of the population.

It has been sometimes assumed almost aprioristically that one of the major distinctions existing today between the religious situation in contemporary Yugoslav society and in some Western European societies is found in the intense process of secularisation and dechristianisation in Yugoslavia, resulting in a far lower general level of commitment to religion and involvement in the church, a process due, for good or bad, to Yugoslavia's socialist system. This may be so if the existing empirical data are taken in a lump together, disregarding regional and local differences. But if the available empirical data are broken down analytically in terms of specific regions and localities and in terms of some specific social strata, then the distinction frequently either disappears altogether or becomes rather unimpressive. For instance, according to some empirical research, the percentage of workers going regularly to Sunday service in church in Bologna, Lyons, and in the region of Paris is lower than the respective percentage for the workers in Zagreb and in the region of Zagreb.[4] The same seems to be valid for data on the commitment to religion of university students in Stockhom or Sweden in general and in some Yugoslav universities.[5] If a list of localities and regions in Europe were drawn up with the most extended disaffection from religion and church, no Yugoslav locality and region with dominant Catholic background would be on the top of that list. Some Italian and French areas would certainly precede the Yugoslav ones.

3. THE YUGOSLAV ANOMALY

The most interesting result that has come out of the still initial empirical research and theoretical investigations points to a phenomenon that may be described as a Yugoslav anomaly if a comparison is made with Western European societies. We recall that it has been one of the first discoveries of sociological theorising and social research on religion that there is a rather stable hierarchy of social classes and strata in respect to their average commitment to religion and their average involvement in the church that has existed for centuries as a massive social fact in the Durkheimian sense. In the social and cultural environment, religion was the only symbolic system establishing the duties and rights of men in society and defining the principles of legitimate social order. It has been found that the lower social classes and more particularly the working class in many European societies lag behind the middle and upper classes in terms of attendance at liturgical rites considered to be religious duties of believers and in terms of their personal religious identification.

F. Isambert has recently shown that according to the research done since World War II the industrial workers of France, more than any other section of the population, remains relatively apart from the Catholic Church.[6] His own studies have established that the religious practice of workers varies considerably from region to region, that it varies in the same direction as does the religious practice of the region's whole population, but that the workers' practice remains always significantly below the general practice.[7] It has also established that there is in many European societies a positive correlation between the level of the commitment to religion and involvement in the church by different social classes and strata and their respective position in the existing social hierarchy, created by the dominant social system and legitimated by the official culture. This is clearly visible in the hierarchy described by J. P. Terrenoire, who distinguished three major groups of the population in France according to their regular dominical practice: at the top of the hierarchy stands the bourgeiosie, agricultural and industrial, including the important agricultural *entrepreneurs,* higher officials, big merchants and the members of free professions: at the bottom there stand the industrial workers and the agricultural hired labour force. The middle classes are located in between, including the small landowners, middle rank officials, clerks, artisans and small merchants.[8] A similar hierarchy seems to be present, at least in France, in the social strata that provide most of the sacerdotal vocations.[9] Ch. Glock and R. Stark come to these general conclusions: 'Lower-classes preference for the this-world solutions associated with radical politics accounts for a considerable portion of the class differences in church attendance,'[10] and 'to the degree that men seek to alter existing stratification arrangements, they are likely to have turned away from the prevailing religious institutions of their societies.'[11]

The Yugoslav 'anomaly' lies in the fact that it is not at all the working class that is located at the bottom of the hierarchy of social strata graded according to their respective commitment to religion and involvement in church, at least in the parts of the country with dominant Roman Catholic tradition. If the commitment to religion and involvement in the church are measured by different indicators generally used in social research, then a hierarchy of social strata can be constructed, going down from the most intensive average commitment to religion and involvement in the church to the least intensive ones. Several studies based upon empirical research have constructed this hierarchy in the following order: (1) peasantry, mostly traditional, but some becoming farmers in the modern sense of the term, (2) self-employed craftsmen and artisans, (3) workers, (4) clerks, (5) intelligentsia and (6) managers and higher officials. And this hierarchy does not change much if different indicators are used, from personal identification in religious terms, attendance to Sunday worship, receiving Communion, church wedding, having one's own children baptised, sending children to catechism, to believing in God, in heaven and hell, etc. If this hierarchy is broken down analytically another step, it appears as follows: (1) peasants, (2) non-qualified and semi-skilled workers, (3) members of free professions, (4) self-employed craftsmen and artisans, (5) skilled workers and craftsmen, (6) low ranking clerks, (7) intelligentsia and (8) managers and higher officials.

This Yugoslav 'anomaly' is confirmed by the social origin of the students at Catholic seminaries and schools of theology. Almost 50 per cent of the students come from peasant families, 40 per cent from working-class families and the remaining 10 per cent from all other social strata. It should be emphasised that this Yugoslav 'anomaly' is of special theoretical interest for two rather different reasons. First, there is no indication that the Church has organised and engaged in intensive pastoral, cultural and pedagogical action specifically directed at the working class or has even tried in a more general way to address the human and social problems of the modern industrial work world. The Church tends to formulate its message by addressing in a general way individuals as such and individuals as members of a nation and a specific culturally defined unit rather than as members of a specific social class facing specific problems in the modern industrial environment. To illustrate this, one could mention that an analysis of the items treated between 1975 and 1978 in the Croatian Catholic magazine *Kana* discloses that problems belonging to the modern industrial working world have been treated very rarely and only in a sporadic way. In these four years only five articles can be listed as dealing in some way with the world of work, compared to 59 devoted to the role of the Church in history in general, 27 to the role of the Church in national history, and 172 to contemporary Church issues.

Secondly, the 'anomaly' is happening in a society in which the official culture of radical secularity constantly insists on the working class as the crucial social class for the life of society and on its further economic growth and social progress. The final conclusion of a general nature derived from these initial theoretical considerations of this problem in the particular Yugoslav context is that commitment to religion and involvement in the church of any social class or stratum are in themselves historical, cultural and social facts, mediated *in concreto* by the complex, dialectical dynamics of social life. This social process, therefore, involves not only quantitative changes of more or less commitment and involvement, but also qualitative changes. This excludes the emergence of a unilinear process either of inevitably progressing secularisation and dechristianisation or of an equally inevitable stabilisation of religion and religious revival, beyond any possibility of reversals and unexpected 'anomalies'.

Notes:

1. For some empirical data see S. Vrcan 'Working-class Commitment to Religion and Society in Yugoslavia' in *C.I.S.R. Actes, 14eme Conférence internationale de sociologie des religions* (Lille 1977) pp. 329-347.

2. See S. Vrcan 'Radnička omladina i religija' in *Poglodi* 4 (1973) 9 125-146.

3. J. Jukić *Religija u modernom industrijakom društvu* (Split 1973) p. 250.

4. Compare the empirical data quoted by F. A. Isambert 'Les Ouvriers et L'Eglise Catholique' in *Revue française de sociologie* 15 (1974) 3 and by G. Michelat and M. Simon *Classe, religion er comportement politique* (Paris 1977) with data in Ś. Bahtijarević and S. Vrcan *Religiozno ponašanje stanovništa zagrebačke regije* (Zagreb 1975).

5. Compare the empirical data adduced by P. Delooz 'Chiesa e società secolarizzata nel'esperienza scandinava,' in *IDOC* 2 (1970) 43 with similar data obtained so far in social research in Yugoslavia.

6. F. A. Isambert in the article cited in note 4.

7. *Ibid.* 532.

8. J. P. Terrenoire 'Groupes socio-professionels et pratiques culturelles catholiques' in *Archives de sciences sociales des religions*, 19 (1974) 37 138.

9. See G. Michelat and M. Simon in the book cited in note 4, *op. cit.*, p. 319.

10. C. Y. Glock and R. Stark *Religion and Society in Transition* (Chicago 1966) p. 197.

11. *Ibid.* p. 202.

PART III

Theological Reflections

Claus Westermann

Work, Civilisation and Culture in the Bible

WHEN we start to consider this subject, we must say a word first of all about the relationship between the Old and New Testaments here. If we were to ask the New Testament alone what it has to say about our subject, the response we should get would be a meagre one. The centre of the New Testament is the message about Christ, and it is so absorbed by this that everything else becomes of merely marginal importance. Moreover, the New Testament came into being in a single century, roughly speaking. The actual time covered by the gospels and the Book of Acts extends over only a few decades. During these years the community of Christians was a group which was on the move, following the disciples, and absorbed in the mission that occupied the first generations of Christians. A comprehensive, intensive encounter between the Christian faith and the culture round it only came about in the course of the Church's history, when it settled down. It was only then that the question of Christianity's relationship to the culture and civilisation surrounding it was raised at all.

The Old Testament is different. It grew up over a period of about a thousand years, and consequently covers the history of God's people both in times when they were on the move and in periods of settlement. Settlement in Canaan brought with it an extremely lively encounter with the civilisation, religion, art and politics of the neighbouring countries, with which the Israelites had to come to terms; this corresponds to the early Church's encounter with *its* surrounding civilisation. All this is reflected in the Old Testament in a number of different ways.

This is the reason why the Old Testament often deals in detail with work and the achievements of civilisation, and why these things are linked in different ways with what God says and does. This applies above all to what the Old Testament has to say about the Creator and creation. Work and civilisation are an essential element in what the Old Testament tells us about both of them.

1. WORK AND CULTURAL ACHIEVEMENT IN THE CONTEXT OF CREATION

In the biblical story about the creation of man (in Genesis 2) man is not created as some ready-made being—simply made, and there he stood—like a statue which one can set up for oneself (though this is the impression given us by the many representations of the creation of man in painting and sculpture). He is created together with his earthly environment, with all its potentialities: space to live in, food, the charge to work and to enjoy companionship. All this belongs to his creation. Without everything that makes his existence possible, his creation would be a pure abstraction. And here the provision of food and the charge to work are closely connected: the Creator provides food for the man he has created by charging him to plant and look after the garden in which he sets him. The plants which feed man grow because the Creator blesses them. But this result of God's blessing is connected with man's own work. The parables of Jesus too link up the Creator's blessing and man's work in the same way.

When the narrator describes the charge to cultivate and look after the fields, he is envisaging arable farming and husbandry. But the charge here is meant in a wider sense. It applies to every form of cultivation, in the widest sense, even to the hunters and 'gatherers'. It is the task entrusted to man together with his living space, and it covers the cultivation and preservation of whatever he has been entrusted with.

The Hebrew verb meaning to cultivate, *'ābad*, corresponds to the Latin *colere*. Like *colere*, it is really transitive and means to cultivate and work *something*. The worker is presented with what he has to work on. The field must be worked. This makes it easier to understand how the Hebrew *'ābad* (like the Latin *colere*) came to have the meaning of serving (God) and why the word used in many languages for 'divine service' (cult, etc.) is derived from this same word. The charge to till the fields is therefore identical here with the command to cultivate in the widest sense: it is a *cultural* charge.

The second word in man's commission means 'to preserve' or 'keep'—the same word which is used for our preservation by God: 'The Lord bless thee and keep thee.' It is not enough to work the ground in order that it may produce something. The fields that have been entrusted to man must be carefully tended and preserved as well. This is intended to exclude from the outset every kind of ruthless exploitation of the ground entrusted to man, with all its natural resources. Any human work which aims solely at output or profit is contrary to God's command if it does not include the preservation and care of the soil.[1]

The two verbs taken together indicate that all human work of whatever kind can participate in the cultivation and preservation of the space which the Creator has given man to live in. Both verbs apply initially only to physical work. The charge does, however, also include mental labour, and the two are of equal value. It is, therefore, impossible to put physical labour on a lower plane than mental exertion. Pleasure in work is founded on the divine commission, which confers dignity on work of every kind; but any idealisation of labour is rejected, because labour too shares in human limitations. All kinds of human labour have their thorns and thistles (Gen. 3:18). Hard labour 'in the sweat of your face' (Gen. 3:19) is involved wherever people work genuinely hard; conquering difficulties is part of the pleasure work gives us.

Genesis 4:17-24 links the command to cultivate and preserve the fields with the genealogy of Cain, because this represents the growth and ramifications of cultivation in its fullest sense. The ploughman is followed by the city-builder (4:17); the nomad, with his sheep and goats, stands beside the tiller of the fields (4:20); his brother is the musician who can play the lyre and pipe (4:21). The father of smiths (or metal-working) is mentioned too. This genealogy presupposes the gradual development of civilised activities. Just as the generations grow up out of the Creator's blessing, so the work of man also grows and branches out; and this growth finds its justification in the Creator's will. The notion of the division of labour is already implicit here.

The biblical view, according to which civilised activity and the growth of mankind both derive from God's blessing, contrasts with the mythical view that the good things and the tools of civilisation are produced by the gods and given to men, or that men were taught these things by gods and cultural heroes.[2] In the myths the works of civilisation are traced back to gods or semi-gods. In the biblical account, on the other hand, it is the power of the Creator's blessing which enables men to grow up to the variety of the civilised activities which spring from that divine power. This means that these civilised activities lose the nimbus of the divine, or of divine origin. Man himself, as God's creation, is empowered by his Creator to create these things. The biblical interpretation also contrasts with the enlightened Greek myth of Prometheus, according to which fire had to be stolen from the gods.[3] In this myth the development of civilisation which fire makes possible is seen in contrast to religion, which was continually losing ground in comparison.

This fundamental biblical statement about work and civilisation was largely overlooked or ignored by Christian tradition, and as a result the further development of civilisation and technology was viewed with distrust by the Christian Churches, instead of being accompanied by thought and prayer. Theology took its bearings from the arts rather than the sciences, in a totally one-sided way. For a long time it wanted to have nothing to do with science and technology. Things are changing now, for the first time; but much too late.

Because this fundamental biblical statement about the development of civilisation was ignored, people were also unable to see that in the same context the Bible draws our attention to the way mankind is endangered through the development of civilisation. This is brought out by the Song of Lamech (Gen. 4:23-24), in which the new technique of fashioning iron makes it possible to produce a weapon of destruction which can serve a brutal will to power. The progress of technology can encourage this will to power to such an extent that it becomes a serious threat to the community of men and women.

The story of the building of the Tower of Babel (Gen. 11:1-9) illustrates another typical threat to the human community through the development of civilisation and technology. Here, with the building of a tower 'with its top in the heavens', building techniques are to serve the striving towards a greatness which reaches out beyond human limitations. Here, at the very beginning of the Bible, it is recognised that human power and greatness in excess can transform the blessing on what man achieves through labour into a curse. It is made plain in the process that an excess of power and greatness which endangers man can proceed from an individual (4:23-24) or a group (11:1-9). At the same time it is recognised that the roots of this excess, and its results, make themselves felt when people live together with people. Lamech wants to show off his power to his wives; the result of the Tower of Babel is that the people concerned can no longer understand one another.

If we see the two things together—the affirmation and the warning—it is evident that the very first pages of the Bible contain clear and unequivocal guidelines for our attitude to work and civilisation. Fundamental mistrust of the progress of human labour in civilisation and technology is just as questionable as blindness to the dangers involved for men and women and the human community in any excess of power and greatness brought about by technological or cultural means.

2. THE UNIQUE CHARACTER OF THE BIBLE'S VIEW OF CIVILISATION

The Bible has no term corresponding to our words 'culture' or 'civilisation'. We can only compare the manifestations of it among ourselves and in the Bible. If we do so, we shall find essential differences. For us 'culture' has almost entirely become a matter of the things of the mind. When we turn to the 'cultural' news in the newspaper, we expect to find reports on science and scholarship, literature, art and the theatre. 'Cultural activities' belong to sectors of life which are very different from the everyday work in the fields, in industry, technology and transport.* Yet it was tilling the fields which was one of the fundamental cultural processes. For culture includes the shaping of tools, the fashioning of metals and the building of houses. The distinction between 'mental' culture and 'manual' culture of a technical or industrial kind is not founded on the biblical view of labour. A real 'humanisation of the world of work' would therefore have to begin with the participation of all human labour in the dignity of cultural activity; and the depreciation of physical labour would have to stop. It is a serious symptom that for us the word 'worker' is still associated with 'lower' kinds of work. No justification can be found in the Bible for the excessive value given to the cultural achievements of the mind, compared with the material achievements of civilisation.

There is another difference as well. Because of the division between material and mental culture, the division between the active and the passive—the people who perform and the public that looks on—has become increasingly dominant. This is true of literature, the visual arts, theatre and music, museums and exhibitions, radio and television. If we ask the Bible about all this, we discover to our astonishment that the people of the Bible knew nothing like this at all. But what we understand by culture today does not have to be culture's sole form. In fact for the men and women of the Bible, culture is something quite different. This requires comprehensive investigation, and I can only give a few examples here.

(1) Culture in the Life of the Community. Let me begin with the visit of the three men to Abraham in Genesis 18. If we read this story carefully and take in its finer points, we realise that the visit of the three men is presented as a cultural event. A visit of this kind was a red-letter day for the nomadic people of that region and period. It stood out from the long days and weeks when they saw no-one. Because it was so special, a meeting of this kind became a festive event, where every gesture, every word and every act had form and style. With exquisite respect and 'courtesy' (though there were no courts as yet) the guests were greeted, invited in, welcomed and given food and drink. In this framework the words that were exchanged took on great importance. It was not a question of 'conversation' in the trivial sense. People really talked to one

* English makes this distinction even crasser by normally using two different words—'culture' and 'civilisation'—for what German identifies under the single term 'Kultur'. It is generally only in historical or anthropological contexts that the English word 'culture' covers the whole civilised activity of the group. (Translator's note)

another. Words exchanged during a visit of this kind were cherished and passed on.

Another example taken from the stories about Abraham is the purchase of Sarah's burial place on her death (Genesis 23). Still another is the wooing of Rebecca (Genesis 24).

(2) In this story Rebecca's brother (her father is already dead) dismisses his sister with a parting blessing, as she goes away to a foreign country: 'Our sister, be the mother of thousands of ten thousands; and may your descendants possess the gate of those who hate them!' The blessing has a rhythmical form. It is a little poem, like many of the Old Testament blessings. The parting is a solemn moment. This poetic utterance turns it into a ceremony which impresses the moment on everyone present. There are little poems like this in many Old Testament stories, at the height of the narrative—for example Adam's cry at the creation of the woman in Genesis 2. Here the 'poem' has a position in the life of a community; it grows out of the situation; and in a situation of this kind anyone can become a poet. The Old Testament has many poems and songs of this kind, which grew up in a similar way out of the life of the community: the work song and the love song, the song of victory, the tribal maxim, and many others. Later there were poems in our sense as well—the work of individual poets. The Book of Job is one. But these are linked with the earlier ones; they do not replace them. The same is true of the stories. Narrative fulfils one of the most important cultural functions in the life of a still illiterate community. It is impossible to develop that here, but the wealth and beauty of the stories in the Old Testament speaks for itself.

(3) The same applies to the historical tradition. There have been few peoples with so strong a sense of history as ancient Israel. History was alive for these people, and everyone shared in it, although there were no historians and no history lessons. Everyone knew the history of his own nation, and much besides. The 'historical creed' is spoken when the offerings are presented (Deuteronomy 26). Gideon, the peasant's son, remembers what God did for his people in former times (Judges 6). During the legal proceedings against Jeremiah (Jeremiah 26), one man can quote the saying of an earlier prophet. The psalms are full of historical reminiscences. This was the foundation which made great historical works possible, like the ones behind the Pentateuch and those describing the kingdom of David.

(4) Culture and Wisdom. A part of the Bible which really has more to do with culture than religion is wisdom. It was only at a relatively late stage that wisdom was taught and learnt; but it grew up before that, out of everyday observation and experience. For ancient Israel, wisdom was one of the most important sectors of cultural activity. Every member of the

nation was potentially involved in it. The wise man approaches an undertaking prudently, taking all the circumstances into account. Wisdom requires a man to know himself and to come to terms with his world—to master the demands life makes on him. Wisdom's main linguistic form—the aphorism—is an expression of the fruits of experience and observation. These aphorisms can pass on experience and help others—for example, 'Better is a little righteousness than great revenues with injustice' (Proverbs 16:8).

Wisdom can be viewed as an early form of philosophy or science. It expresses the searching and questioning of the human spirit, which looks into the world and man. But here the observation of phenomena is not something isolated and abstract, as it is in the empirical sciences. It is closely bound up with experience, which requires a growth and maturity of perception. Experiment is not enough. In order to acquire wisdom we must experience life's heights and depths. The fact that wisdom restricts itself to what is necessary and essential is another sign of its humanity. In contrast to the differentiations of the sciences, Old Testament wisdom emphasises whatever binds all human knowledge together, and what men and women can have in common.

(5) Culture in the Image. A sub-category of the aphorism is the aphorism of comparison, e.g., 'Like a gold ring or an ornament of gold is a wise reprover to a listening ear' (Proverbs 25:12). The comparison presents our concept of what is valuable by comparing the wise warning of a person of forethought, whose warning is observed, with the gift of a piece of costly jewellery. The comparison makes its effect by showing a connection between two different spheres of existence; the way in which the two comparable things are expressed makes the aphorism a verbal work of art. In these comparisons, and in the other aphorisms as well, the whole civilisation of the villages and towns of ancient Israel come alive: the towns with their walls and towers; the villages with their houses and little streets; the work in the fields, the work of the craftsmen, and much else. There is a profusion of these aphorisms of comparison. They belong to the wider field of metaphors, images and parables in the Old and New Testaments. What they express is not simply the wish to make abstract things vivid but, in talking about man, to let man's world have its say. The reality which surrounds people and which is familiar to them is intended to make what is said about man and his relationship to God clearer and more convincing. Unlike a mathematical equation, every apt verbal comparison is a work of art. The visual arts—painting and sculpture—play practically no part in the Bible; their place is taken by the verbal comparison, which was enormously richly developed.

This is particularly true of Jesus' parables in the New Testament. It is only when we see these against the background of the similes, metaphors and comparative aphorisms in the Old Testament that it becomes clear that they deal very largely with what we call civilisation and culture. Jesus' parables show a keen appreciation of this part of life. The correspondence between different things which is expressed here means that man's labour and his civilisation and culture are included when we talk about God's activity. In this way Jesus includes these aspects of life in the total happening between God and man, the Creator and his creation—which of course is in line with the divine charge to work given in the creation narrative.

We could say much more about the cultural importance of the language of the Bible. It is perhaps the Bible's greatest cultural achievement that its simple language should have remained comprehensible throughout the course of several thousand years and in spite of many linguistic and cultural barriers.

3. PARTICIPATION IN THE CULTURAL ACHIEVEMENTS OF OTHERS

What the primeval history has to say about work, the way it develops and all its ramifications, applies to the labour of people everywhere. This means that work and the achievements of civilisation are founded on the Creator's will, together with the whole of mankind itself. Consequently the Bible talks without any reserve or embarrassment about the way the people of God took over the cultural achievements of other nations.

The most important of these achievements was writing. Writing is one of the most vital cultural achievements in the history of man. It was invented outside Israel and had been considerably developed before Israel adopted it. It was writing that made the Bible as a book possible. This fact shows clearly enough that cultural achievements could be welcomed and adopted even when they grew up outside Israel and her religion.

We could develop this further. The original language of the Scriptures, the language of God's Word, in which the Lord proclaimed to the Israelites, 'I have seen the affliction of my people', had the long and complicated linguistic history of the Semitic languages behind it. And this history was enacted outside Israel's history and religion. The words for what happened between God and Israel were not created for that purpose in the first place. They were taken over from elsewhere. Consequently the language itself is no more sacred than the characters in which it is written. Both the language and writing of the Old Testament participated in a cultural development which extended far beyond Israel and its history. The same is true of the language and writing of the New Testament—even more so, indeed; for the language spoken by Jesus and his disciples is cut off from the language and script of the New Testament by the frontier dividing two linguistic families. Language and writing make it especially clear that no religion can be independent of general cultural development. There is always some recognition of the work and civilisation outside one's own religion, even if only to a limited degree.

There are many other areas of culture where we can see adoptions of this kind in the Bible. This is less evident as long as the religion is just a movement, like Christianity at the time of Jesus and the apostles. Massive adoption begins when religion becomes established. The Old Testament makes this clear. When it settled down in Canaan, Israel adapted its law to the legal systems of the Middle East. Here too the cultural achievements of others were able to serve the people of Israel and this fact was given recognition when they were combined with 'God's law'. Something similar took place when Roman law was accepted by the Christian nations. The people of Israel developed no architecture of their own. Not only did they take over the construction of houses and city fortifications from the Canaanites, Solomon actually employed Canaanite architects for the temple in Jerusalem. This was very important, because cultic elements were taken over from Canaan as well as the architecture and ornaments.

Moreover it is possible to talk about a religious culture which goes far beyond individual religions, both geographically and in time. Israel found the practice of sacrifice already in existence and took it over, as Genesis 4 and 8 show. It did not adopt it in response to its God's command. Seasonal festivals are widespread, since they grow up out of an agricultural way of life. They were taken over by both the Israelite and Christian religions, though with a new significance. Certain kinds of worship, too, are common to many religions: for example, meeting together in a big building, with fixed gestures, acts and words. But the opposite is true as well. Many religious elements penetrate non-religious culture and go on existing there as cultural elements. We need only remember that temples and churches are the documents of cultural development as well, and that museums all over the world are full of objects and works of art which originally had religious significance. There are many linguistic features too whose religious origin has been forgotten, or which we are no longer aware of. One of many is the word 'sacrifice'. The Russian word for Sunday means 'resurrection', while the words 'to thank' mean 'to reverence'.

This intertwining of religion and culture makes participation in cultural achievements outside one's own religion possible in the Bible too. But it raises a number of questions which have hardly been thought about sufficiently up to now. To mention only one: the New Testament shows us that a flood of Greek words and ways of thinking were absorbed into the language and thought of the early Church. Does this mean that these cultural loans are to hold good permanently?

4. THE BIBLE'S CRITICISM OF THE OVERVALUATION OF CIVILISATION AND CULTURE

We may begin with what we have just said: Israel was able to make the temple in Jerusalem a religious centre which was reverenced and loved by the whole people, as the 'Zion' psalms show. Yet at the same time it was possible for the prophets Micah and Jeremiah to prophesy the destruction of that temple, as a divine judgment. The temple had no absolute religious value; and its cultural value could not save it once it was misused. This makes it emphatically clear that work and culture, even in the religious field, cannot take on independent value.

(1) Jesus rejects the undue importance given to work in the parable of the rich farmer (Luke 12:13-41). This parable rejects the widespread opinion that work, and work well done, can make life secure. But in this parable Jesus does not contrast work with 'higher values'. He is quite down-to-earth; he points to death: 'Fool! This night your soul is required of you.' The saying about worry in the Sermon on the Mount belongs to the same context. Here Jesus points to the Creator who looks after what he has made.

(2) These two sayings of Jesus acquire their full significance only in the light of what the first chapter of the Bible has to say indirectly about work. The six days of creation lead up to the seventh, on which the Creator 'rests from his labours'. This is a declaration that work is only one part of a bigger whole; rest is the other part. The seventh day is no longer allocated to the working days, as the day of rest that is necessary for work's sake. It has its own purpose, which goes beyond what work can achieve. In the Priestly Document, the day on which God rests points forward to the institution of worship; the rhythm of weekdays and holidays points beyond itself to the whole of human life, whose goal is not the performance of work, but something beyond that, which is indicated in God's 'resting'. The universal conception at the beginning of the Bible makes it clear that, biblically speaking, work is not an ultimate value in itself. For the Bible there can be no glorification of labour as life's meaning and fulfilment. On the other hand, the Sabbath commandment says equally clearly: 'Six days you shall labour.' That is to say, the greater part of the time granted to man is to be devoted to work. The Sabbath commandment is also significant because it preserves the rhythm of working days and holidays, and because it embodies God's charge to man to work.

(3) The overvaluation of culture and civilisation that is criticised in Genesis 4 and 11 applies to mankind as a whole. The prophets picked it up and applied it to Israel, God's people, in their attack on social conditions. This attack has hardly ever been seriously listened to in Christian tradition. In their accusations the prophets passionately resist any evalu-

ation of cultural values and achievements which ignores the way these came into being. They are firmly opposed to seeing anything as beautiful or splendid or noble if it has been achieved at the cost of oppression and injustice:

> Woe to him who builds a town with blood,
> and founds a city on iniquity!
> For the stone will cry out from the wall,
> and the beam from the woodwork respond (Hab. 2:12 and 11).

Here we must mention the poem of Isaiah's which proclaims the downfall of the works of human arrogance (Isa. 2:6-22) as well as Jeremiah's attack on the king 'who builds his house by injustice' (22:13-17), the frequent attacks on the luxury of the rich, which has been acquired by oppressing the man in the street, and many other sayings. What they all have in common is that here an abstract evaluation of a cultural achievement is sharply condemned in God's name, if it has been won through oppression and injustice.

We might well go on to ask more questions here, for this aspect too has hardly been given sufficient attention in the traditions of the Christian church. What the Bible says about the social and theological aspect of civilisation and culture differs in a number of ways from our ideas, which go back essentially to the Greek and Roman world, which the young Church grew up into. That was possible as long as Christianity was largely confined to the area of this particular civilisation. Now we are being forced to think ecumenically here too. We should look more closely at the points where our view of civilisation and cultural achievement deviates from the Bible. One of these points is the sharp objectification of civilisation, which has been encouraged by the division into the producers and the consumers of its products. Another point is our concept of education, which has made it possible to divide people into 'the educated' and 'the uneducated'. A third point is the supremacy of an élite, which goes back to the objective value ascribed to culture in itself. In all these matters the prophets' criticism of the greatness of a civilisation in abstraction from the concrete ways in which it was built up can be of help to us.

Translated by Margaret Kohl

Notes

1. We cannot enter into the wider ecological complex here, but see G. Liedke *Im Bauche des Fisches, Ökologische Theologie* (Stuggart, Berlin 1979).
2. See *Biblischer Kommentar, Neukirchen*, I, 1 *Genesis* (1974) p. 463ff.
3. See in this connection P. Audet 'La Revanche de Promothée ou le drame de la religion et de la culture' *Revue Biblique* 73 (1966) 5-29.

Francis Schüssler Fiorenza

Religious Beliefs and Praxis: Reflections on Catholic Theological Views of Work

CRITICAL reflection means becoming aware of the interrelation between theory, praxis, and interest. A theory unaware of its relation to praxis or its inherent interests is a theory blind to its own presuppositions, consequences, and driving forces. If theology is to become critically self-conscious, it must analyse the presuppositions, consequences, and interests of its theoretical affirmations. This critical reflection upon the interrelation between theory and praxis is especially necessary for theological reflections about the meaning of work, for religious beliefs and social praxis have been nowhere so intextricably intertwined as in regard to work. Nevertheless, this interrelation has often gone unexamined. The causes and consequences of certain religious attitudes towards work and of theological views about the meaning of work have often been neglected and overlooked, even by authors producing a theology of work.

Therefore, the modern attempts at a theology of work need to be critically examined. It is necessary to see their historical background and to examine the historical tradition within its social context and praxis. This essay, therefore, seeks to point out the interrelation between religious beliefs and praxis by reflecting upon Catholic theological views of work. Its goal is limited in two ways. Firstly, the criticisms of how the attempts at a theology of work have elaborated the meaning of work do not imply that all Catholic theology has inadequately analysed work. In fact, much of recent Catholic social teaching, especially contemporary papal and episcopal documents, has critically focused upon the social and economic praxis of work. Secondly, these critical observations are not offered as a comprehensive survey either of the various conceptions of a theology of work or of the meaning of work itself.[1]

We shall follow the following approach. 1. We shall first survey three distinct theological reflections upon work that have been influential within Catholic theology. 2. Secondly, we shall refer these reflections to their historical contexts and examine their adequacy to our contemporary societal situation. 3. Finally, as a result, it will be suggested that a theology of work is inadequate unless it considers both the ambivalence of religious attitudes towards work and the ambiguity of work itself. Intrinsic to any theology of work is, therefore, an appropriate application of the religious tradition, an insight into the structures of power and domination within the work situation, and the conjunction of a theology of work with practical reason.

1. THREE THEOLOGICAL REFLECTIONS ON WORK

1. *Work as Personal and Social Fulfilment*

In reaction to Max Weber's interpretation of the relation of the reformation to capitalism and the rationalisation of modern society, Catholic scholars have re-examined the work ethic of the medieval period.[2] Although their reaction sometimes misreads Weber's thesis, they have provided very useful comprehensive accounts of the medieval notion of work. For example, Thomas Aquinas had previously been interpreted almost exclusively from the section in the *Summa* (*ST*, 2a-2ae, 187, 3) where work is described in four ways: (1) a means of livelihood; (2) a remedy against idleness, the source of evil; (3) a bridle of the concupiscence of the flesh; and (4) a source for almsgiving. But this evaluation of work expresses solely his views in regard to the obligation of manual labour for religious orders. As such it represents only one aspect of the medieval attitude toward work.[3]

Human work and human vocations are seen within a theocentric, organic, and universalistic view of the universe.[4] As every other creature, human beings fit into the order of the universe. They not only fit into God's plan, but also cooperate in bringing it to consummation.[5] In the divine plan, human work has a social and communal dimension. Individuals depend upon one another and upon society. They perform services for others, and they expect a reciprocal return. Even if the individual's intention (*finis operantis*) is selfish, the objective purpose of work (*finis operis*) is ordered to the community. When the subjective intention and the objective purpose totally coincide, then work is properly done. Work is therefore a task, an office, and an obligatory service which individuals perform for each other and the community.[6]

The belief in divine providence undergirds this harmony since it maintains the balance between the community's needs and the individual's inclinations. God arranges and pre-orders a correspondence between an individual's inclination for a particular job and the specific needs of the whole community.[7] This divinely ordained coincidence means that a person's vocation in life is not only divinely ordered, but also insures that the individual's person fulfilment is at the same time the community's fulfilment. Persons fulfil themselves in meeting the needs of the community. Individual natural inclinations and vocational fulfilment do not therefore stem merely from natural factual contingencies, as Max Weber asserted of the medieval position,[8] but flow from the divine will. God wills the diverse inclinations as well as the different vocations. Therefore, divine providence accords a religious significance to a person's inclinations, status, and vocational occupation.

The same view appears in medieval sermons. In his sermon on the ten choirs of angels, Berthold von Regensburg explains that God has willed both the various vocations and the different ranks of society. Each person has a specific social position and a definite vocational task just as each of the ten choirs of angels do. God wills every vocation and social position. This medieval view attributes meaning to each person's status and vocation. It is at the same time a religious legitimation and a theological justification of vocational and social distribution.

2. *Work as Discipline and Achievement*

In the seventeenth and eighteenth centuries a development in the religious evaluation of work takes place that serves as a precursor of the bourgeois and middle class conception of work.[9] During this period, the Jansenist and Jesuit attitude toward work and life form a link to the development of the bourgeois conception. Their views provide the religious background to those attitudes that will be developed by the middle class.

The Jansenist mentality, exemplified by Pierre Nicole's *Essais de morale*,[10] appealed to Christian principles to regulate even the smallest details of life. Individuals are first of all Christians and pilgrims on earth. Their election to eternity and not their status in the world is important. This divine favour is seen not so much in the rich and powerful as in the middle class and especially in their fidelity to obligations, their dedication to hard work, and their earnest and self-sufficient attitude toward life. These virtues eventually become distinctive of the middle class. The Jansenist emphasis that Christian morality was principally human action was a preparation for the development of the middle class mentality.

The Jesuit position, exemplified by Louis Bourdaloue's sermons,[11] provided another element. They gave the middle class an awareness of its particular role in society. Whereas the Jansenists underscored the individual's autonomy from the general values of society, the Jesuits correlated virtue and social order. God willed the particular vocations and different ranks. Individuals were to be educated to perform their specific offices in life.

Baroque theology and popular sermons spoke of the Christian obligation to work. Jesus worked. He is the model for Christians. Nevertheless the reasons and motives for working are important to the conception of work. The Jansenist literature praised those very aspects of work which we might consider its negative qualities. They praise work precisely because it is difficult, weary, monotonous, necessary, and strenuous. Work unmasks the vanity of the world. It undercuts the human desire for pleasure. Seen in the context of the divine plan, work has a positive meaning in so far as it serves as a penance for sins. Like sickness and suffering, work results from sin. But by turning us away from the vanity of the world, it aids human beings in the glorification of God.

This religious conception of work forms the background to the emergence of a new understanding within the middle class. The bourgeois conception goes beyond this religious conception of work as a penitential discipline to a view of work as a means of success and a positive constructive task.

The transition is important. In the religious conception, work is not meaningful in itself as an end. It has meaning in so far as it demands an industrious orderly life, an ascetic self-discipline and a methodic control of the details of life. Jesuit discipline trained individuals in the subjection of life to order, rules and self-observation. It therefore provided a background training for the middle class and its life orientation.

Nevertheless a difference exists. The religious evaluation of work as a distraction from the vanity of life or as the disciplined, methodic regulation of life does not completely correspond to the emerging bourgeois conception of work as constructive. Work can be understood as a penance for sins by the poor, but not by the bourgeois who profit and advance through work. Work brings success, riches, and respect. It is also an accomplishment and an achievement. The bourgeois attitude grows out of this religious evaluation, but goes beyond it.[12] It is mainly at a later period in history that theologians will attempt to elaborate theologically this bourgeois conception and apply it to all social groupings.

3. *Work as Participation in Divine Creativity*

The 1950s witness the emergence of several attempts to develop a theology of work.[13] They approach the distinctively bourgeois conception of work, even though they are not unaware that the modern industrial experience challenges this very conception. In fact their very starting-point presupposes that industrialisation with its mass production and its assembly lines had led to the loss of the human significance of work.

This development is seen as negative both in itself and in its consequences for Christianity. M. D. Chenu writes in his influential *The Theology of Work*: 'Work no longer had any human significance and so could not have a religious one.' As human beings became estranged in their work, they became estranged from their God. As they lost themselves in work, they lost their God. The remedy, he suggests, should be neither political nor moral, but theological. The integrity of work must be restored. The task is 'theologically speaking, to re-establish work in its cosmic and human functions, and in the design of God the Creator'.[14]

Therefore, theology must appropriate the Christian tradition to give meaning to work within the modern situation. A theology of work is therefore to be developed that stresses several positive themes about work. Firstly, according to Christian revelation human beings are commanded by God to master the material universe. According to Genesis this command is the basic human vocation. Through domination over nature, human beings participate in the divine creativity. Technology and industrialisation do not lessen or impede this domination but further it. Hence industrialisation enables humans to further collaborate in God's creativity. Secondly, Christian anthropology teaches that human beings are not just externally juxtaposed bodies and souls, since body and soul interpenetrate. Consequently, in so far as human work conjoins human free will and material technology, it extends the reality of human nature and creativity. Finally, the economy of salvation and incarnation do not imply the annihilation of the material world, but rather its transformation and incorporation into the order of grace. Work should be seen as a part of this transformation and integration.

Chenu's theology of work looks toward the positive and objective. To understand the reality of modern work, he argues, one must not stop at the detrimental psychological effects of work but concentrate on the transformation and integration of life by work. In this encounter between human beings and nature, work is not primarily a discipline or a perfection of the worker through his (her) work.[15] The meaning of work lies in its objectivity and creativity. The meaning of work lies within the work itself. It has its own value and integrity in the formation of the world, quite independently of the detrimental or constructive effect it may have on the worker. The objectivity of work, therefore, points to the intrinsic creativity and productivity of human labour. This is the divine command to humans and the meaning of the basic vocation to work.

2. THE HISTORICAL SOCIAL CONTEXT

Although each of these three conceptions of work (as a specific place in divinely ordered universe, as a discipline and a means of success, and as a creative activity) have specific historical contexts, they coalesce in many theological treatments of work. Often one or the other element is stressed, e.g., work as a difficult discipline or work as creative; often several notions are combined together, e.g., work as a divine vocation and work as creative. Nevertheless, each of these three religious attitudes toward work should be examined in the light of their historical matrix and in reference to the contemporary social situation.

The medieval view of work within a divinely ordered universe in which natural inclination and vocational opportunity coincide was elaborated in a society where vocational mobility was limited. Persons had a particular status and place in society. The theology of work as a theology correlating natural inclination and vocational opportunities religiously justified this social order. But is it not inappropriate, to say the least, in modern society where an increasing discrepancy exists between educational training and vocational opportunity? Is it also not inappropriate to a dynamic, and often dysfunctional market situation that demands vocational mobility, temporary joblessness, and vocational retraining? The dedication to a specific vocational task becomes a handicap to the psychological and social readjustments necessary today. If it can be questioned whether religion should justify social status and vocational task, it is even more doubtful whether this should be done in a situation demanding mobility.

The conception of work as an ascetic discipline stood in the background of the emergence of the middle class. Here the religious praise of the discipline of work with its hardships and its orderly regulation of life reinforced the discipline needed for work. The religious conception of work as a punishment for sin, as a remedy against pursuit of pleasure, and as a sign of the vanity of the world rang true for the poor who worked in order to survive. But for the middle class, the discipline of work no longer served as a distraction from the glories of the world but became a means of success and a constructive task.

The modern theology of work attempts to give meaning to work precisely at a time when it appears to have become meaningless through industrialisation. Its hope that industrialisation will further the creative and productive purpose within human nature overlooks the fragmentation of work that has occurred. This is obvious in Chenu's comparison of modern technology with the discovery of the horse collar in the Middle Ages.[16] Whereas the horse collar increased the productivity of draught animals and thereby liberated human beings for higher values and work, the effect of industrialisation and the assembly line should be to increase both productivity and communality among workers.

Not only can the optimistic interpretation of technology and industrialism be questioned, but it can also be disputed whether a theology of work is adequate if it attempts to give meaning to work mainly by the theological application of religious beliefs to work. Does not such an attempt overlook the societal interests and concrete economics involved in the specific quality and situation of work? Is not such a theology of work an attempt at legitimation in so far as it seeks to give work a meaning that was previously shared by the bourgeois or the intellectual strata of society but never by all members of society?[17]

3. THEOLOGY AND SOCIAL PRAXIS

The questions raised in regard to each of these three traditions point to the necessity of establishing the limits and parameters of any theology of work. Therefore, instead of elaborating a theology of work, several conditions should be outlined as imperatives of theological reflection on work.

Firstly, it is essential to reflect upon the ambivalence and ambiguity of work both within the religious tradition and within societal praxis. In the religious tradition, work has both a positive and a negative evaluation. It is seen as creative, as a service to community, and as a divine vocation. Yet it is also negatively evaluated as a punishment for sin. In contemporary society, a similar ambivalence exists. On the one hand, work is seen as important for the individual's self-concept, sense of fulfilment, and integration into society. On the other hand, there is an increasingly instrumentalistic attitude toward work: persons work not so much for the sake of the work itself, but for the rewards of work.[18] Likewise a split often exists between professional-vocational life and private-personal life. A duality exists between professional training and vocational opportunities due to the changes in the market situation and the dynamics of the educational system.

Secondly, if this ambivalence both in religious beliefs and societal praxis is taken into account, then the criterion of the appropriateness of application becomes intrinsic to the theoretical formation of a theology of work. Application is not merely supplemental to theory. An abstract theology of work can be put to ideological use or used to satisfy ideological needs. Theological affirmations of the positive meaningful nature of work can serve to minimise the *de facto* negative qualities of work with its dehumanising fragmentation. It can overlook the lot of the poor, of men and women on the assembly line and in impersonal service positions. Yet this very theological affirmation of the positive meaning of work can also serve as an ideal which judges this present fragmentation. It can be the symbolic and conceptual force behind a societal critique.

The same dialectic operates for the negative religious affirmations of work. It can justify the injustices and inhumanity of the work situation. If work is a punishment for sin or if work is the sad lot of our fallen state, then one should not expect any reform of the conditions of work. After all work is work and no reform can place paradise on earth.[19] On the other hand, the negative religious evaluations of work can help persons survive in social structures, in which work is alienating or unemployment an economic spin-off of the fight against inflation. This negative religious evaluation reinforces the instrumentalist attitude toward work and therefore can give people an independence and autonomy in the face of an otherwise hopeless reality.

Thirdly, a theology of work should be conjoined with practical reason if it is to elaborate the meaning of work not as a concrete ideology, but as symbolic belief in emancipation and redemption. This necessity does not only lie in the ambivalence of religious beliefs toward work and in the ambiguity of work itself, but also in the relation of work to the organisation of society. Work is not merely a vocational occupation. Nor is it merely a technical mastery of nature. But work is essential to human and social interaction. Human society and interaction consists not only of language, but also of work and power. In so far as power and authority determine human interaction, questions of domination and exploitation have shaped the meaning of work. Therefore, language about work has been determined by the structures of power and domination.[20]

It is therefore necessary for theology to reflect upon how societal structures of domination have not only affected the conditions of work, but have permeated the religious evaluation of work in concrete situations. The unity of theoretical and practical reason, which is an essential condition for a theology of work, is secured only if the religious interpretation of work is conjoined with a discussion of the distribution, structure, and rewards for work within society. Its purpose would be to insure that neither the positive nor the negative religious evaluation of work is given an ideological function, but rather can be appropriated to serve the emancipation of human beings within the work situation and the transformation of the work situation itself.

Questions of the distribution, structures, and rewards for work are therefore not incidental, but crucial to the theological evaluation of work. In a society with a division of labour, the quality of work opportunities vary just as do the rewards. How is the distribution of tasks to be made? As a rule the harsh tasks have been distributed not merely to the unskilled, but to the powerless or the poor who have no other option. For a theology of work, the crucial question then becomes whether religious values reinforce or hinder an unequal, exploitative or oppressive distribution of labour. In the eighteenth century, the notion of divine providence was used to justify a *laissez-faire* attitude toward the free market and its distribution.[21] The religious sanctioning of patriarchal marriage has not only excluded women from certain types of work, but reinforced their working without financial rewards.[22] The image of an ordered society has served to explain the inequalities of positions and rewards. The challenge for a theology of work is then how it can avoid serving this function. How can it have a critical and emancipatory function?[23]

Theology must combine religious vision and practical reason. Questions about the distributions of work are often not posed in terms of exploitation, oppression, or injustice. But are treated abstractly as technical issues: how does one balance the advantages of the fragmentation of labour for productivity and efficiency in industrial, clerical, and service areas with its dehumanising effects on the workers? How does one balance the rights of individuals for meaningful employment with the interest in being competitive on the international market by curbing inflation and opting for higher rates of unemployment? How does one balance equity and growth? The solution to these dilemmas does not lie merely in pragmatic or strategic answers, but rests upon images of society and of human life.

These images of society and of human life are at the centre of religious beliefs with their transcendent and Utopian affirmation. The transcendence of these affirmations prohibits that one reduce questions of social life to merely technical issues. The transcendent ideal must be conjoined with the demands of practical reason, worked out in free, open discourse so that the application of the religious images and values does not become an ideology.

The issues of the conflict between meaningfulness and competitiveness, between individual rights and economic advancement, and between equity and growth are therefore not simply pragmatic problems, but issues about the public meaning and significance of the religious vision of an eschatological society of justice and peace. Only through this combination of religious vision and practical discourse does a theology of work avoid becoming an ideology of work. It becomes a critical and self-reflective theology of work if it understands the meaning of human work within the context of a theory of society, in which transcendent values of love and justice should become immanent and prevail.

Notes

1. See F. S. Fiorenza 'Work and Critical Theology' in *A Matter of Dignity* ed W. J. Heisler, J. W. Houck (Notre Dame 1977) pp. 23-44. For the most recent and comprehensive encyclopedia article see 'Arbeit' in *Theologische Realenzyklopädie* II pp. 613-669.

2. N. Paulus 'Die Wertung der weltlichen Berufe in Mittelalter' *Hist. Jahrbuch der Goerresgesellschaft* 32 (1911) 725-755, and 'Der Berufsgedanke bei Thomas von Aquin' *Zeitschrift für katholische Theologie* 50 (1926) 445-454; see Tranquilli 'Il concetto di lavore in S. Tommaso d'Aquino' *Rivista Trimestrale* 4 (1963) 664-700.

3. It is important to divide the medieval attitudes toward work into quite distinct periods: see J. LeGoff *Le Travail dans la France médiévale* ed. M. François (Paris 1972) pp. 296-347.

4. The Stoic metaphor of the body as an organism was borrowed by Paul (I Cor. 12:4-31) to explain the diversity of charisms in the church. It is now applied to society in general: see A. H. Chroust 'The Corporate Idea and the Body Politic in the Middle Ages' *Review of Politics* 9 (1947) 423-452.

5. *Summa contra gentiles* 3.77; see also 69f. 113; *Compendium Theologiae* 1.148.

6. *Summa Theologica, Suppl.* 41.2.

7. *Summa Theologica* 2a-2ae 183.2; *Summa contra gentiles* 3.134; *Quodlibet* 7 and 12; *Contra impugnantes* 5.

8. Max Weber *The Protestant Ethic and the Spirit of Capitalism*, trans. T. Parsons (New York 1920, 1958) p. 80. See also K. Holl *Aufsätze zur Kirchengeschichte* (Tübingen 1978) III pp. 189-219; K. Dunkmann *Die Lehre vom Beruf* (Berlin 1922). They appeal especially to *Queastiones quodlibetates* 7, art. 17c, as support for a naturalistic interpretation. For the contrary, see *Summa contra gentiles* 3.134; 'Now this division of various jobs among different persons is done by divine providence inasmuch as some people are more inclined to one kind of work than another.'

9. B. Groethusen *Die Entstehung der bürgerlichen Welt- und Lebensanschauung in Frankreich* (Frankfurt 1978) 2. For later development in the eighteenth and nineteenth centuries see A. Clayre *Work and Play* (New York 1974).

10. See Le Breton-Grandmaison *Pierre Nicole ou la civilité chrétienne* (Paris 1945).

11. See 'Sermon sur l'oisivite' Migne, *Coll. integr. et univ. des orateurs chrétiens*, I vol. XVII.

12. It is interesting that in the nineteenth century, liberalism optimistically evaluated work because it coordinated work and freedom, whereas conservative movements as well as socialism pointed out the negative aspects of the present conditions of work.

13. H. Rondet 'Elements pour une théologie du travail' *Nouvelle Revue Theologique* 77 (1955) 27-48 and 123-143; J. Lacroix 'La notion de travail' *La Vie Intellectuelle* (June 1952) 4-31; M. D. Chenu *The Theology of Work* (1955) (Dublin 1963); J. H. Oldham *Work in Modern Society* (Richmond 1950, 1961);

A. Auer *Christsein in Beruf* (Düsseldorf 1966); J. J. Illanes *On the Theology of Work* (Chicago 1967); E. Kaiser *Theology of Work* (Westminster, Md. 1966).

14. Quotations from Chenu *The Theology of Work* at p. 16.

15. *Ibid.* 19. Although I criticise Chenu's theological conception of work in the following pages, he is more aware than others of the negative qualities of industrialised labour.

16. *Ibid.*

17. See J. B. Gilbert *Work Without Salvation* (Baltimore 1977); D. T. Rodger *The Work Ethic in Industrial America 1850-1920* (Chicago 1978).

18. See H. Wilensky 'Work as a Social Problem' *Social Problems: A Modern Approach* ed. H. S. Becker (New York 1966).

19. Noteworthy is Karl Barth's analysis of work and capitalist competition: see *Church Dogmatics* III, part 4, sect. 55.

20. See the critique of Karl Rahner by M. Moser and P. G. Schervish 'Theology of Work: A Liberation Perspective' *Radical Religion* 3 (1978) 30-36.

21. See P. D. Anthony *The Ideology of Work* (London 1977).

22. J. Viner *The Role of Providence in the Social Order* (Princeton 1972).

23. L. A. Tilly and J. W. Scott *Women, Work, and Family* (New York 1978).

24. For this question, see F. S. Fiorenza 'Critical Social Theory and Christology' *Proceedings of the Catholic Theological Society of America* 30 (1975) 63-110 and 'Political Theology as Foundational Theology' *Ibid.* 32 (1977) 142-177.

Silvano Burgalassi

Towards a Theology of Man as Worker

AN effective consideration of 'a theology of man as worker' is, it seems to me, only possible if it takes account of the joint interaction of three component elements:

(i) Theological reflection (speaking of God or with God), generally formulated on the basis of Old or New Testament revelation, on the work of major theologians (patristic or scholastic), the directives of the Magisterium (encyclicals) and the practice of the Church;

(ii) Analysis of the different forms taken by *work* in the past; this has in fact, till now, generally meant conditions of work at the time the Bible texts were compiled (nomadic, agricultural and artisan) and medieval practices;

(iii) A certain (somewhat limited) amount of attention paid to the subjective or objective condition of the protagonists of work, the workers, seen in their actual operations rather than in learned reflection on their work produced by cultured individuals who are—probably—incapable of understanding the full implications of work conditions.

Almost all theological analyses of work clearly take most account of the first two 'modes', and put the first way above the second, while hardly even hinting at the existence of the third. The consequence of this anomalous type of approach is that theological reflection, starting with the Bible and taking the elements it applies to the objective reality of today almost exclusively from this, is liable to end up chasing its own tail, reflecting only on itself and ignoring the 'existential conditions of work' which are precisely what theology ought to be trying to interpret. It would seem that theology ought to take another course: to start with the real conditions of workers and then go on to see how these make it possible (or perhaps easier) to use the aids provided by theological and religious data in order to arrive at a coherent Christian view.

1. NOMADISM AND THE THEOLOGY OF THE TRANSITORY NATURE OF THINGS

The first hominids found on earth, some two and a half million years ago (compared to the 50,000 years to the first traces of *Homo sapiens*) show signs of belonging to the 'social' category of *nomadic hunters*, later becoming nomadic pastors when they discovered the possibility of domesticating animals. If one can talk of 'work roles' in such a situation, the only activity undertaken in small groups (hardly ever more than twenty-thirty persons) was the very limited one of hunting and fishing, which were vital to physical survival. Apart from that, time was given over to feasting, play, dance and ritual. One might say that every day was a feast day, whereas work and the supplying of needs were a minor interval, in both time and importance, dictated only by biological survival.[1]

Ritual, i.e., *collective reflection* on the meaning of life, through remembrance of the past (myth) and anticipation of the future (*eschaton*), in such a situation takes on its basic importance as reflective or conscientising *meditation*, thereby becoming that 'second nature' which was later to emerge as culture. Even if it is exaggerated to speak of a theology of *nomadism* when referring to a cultural stage when theological reflection only took place on the most elementary level, this type of life nevertheless gave rise to some basic tenets of revealed religion and particularly of the Christian religion: the *transitory* nature of life symbolised by the tent in the desert; faith in God based on the uncertainty of tomorrow; a certain cosmic fatalism derived from man's impotence in the face of the forces of nature; disdain for the *settled life*, which still characterises several cultures today; the feeling for *rowdy festivals* which carried on until recent times and is still found in folklore and revivalist meetings. These 'archetypal traits' form elements still found—though maybe latent—in the mental make-up of nomadic populations today (such as the Kuchi, the Tuaregs, the Gypsies) and of the neo-nomads produced by the social mobility brought about by ease of transportation.

2. AGRICULTURE AND CRAFTS: THE THEOLOGY OF CYCLIC STATICITY

With the transition from nomadic life—hunting, breeding, fishing—to an agricultural culture, starting in the eighth millennium B.C. and completed within two thousand years, individual and community life was completely changed. The vital element, once the women (probably) had discovered reproduction of crops from seed, became being *rooted* to the soil, usually to the same patch of soil, which gave rise to the extended family and then to the need to form permanent relationships with other families, producing the village. The village, writing, the cart wheel, the first rudiments of science, the birth of the great salvation religions, all date from this epoch. Tilling the soil offered a new model of social life, centred on the patriarchal model of the extended family.[2]

In the family as such, everyone had a particular role, biological and economic, thereby making it a sort of 'cost-reducing enterprise' through the effective carrying-out of social tasks. Among these tasks, those most highly regarded were those that could be carried out in the home or near it (husbandry, craftwork), and the home came to assume a quite new importance.

Agricultural labour provides the basic elements for survival where there is a continual natural generosity (hence the cult of Mother Earth, ever fertile as women are), but imposes some requirements such as strict observance of the seasons (for sowing, cultivating, harvesting and storing), and tends to produce a certain fatalism, inherent in work that consists largely of waiting for the harvest, the element most necessary for survival, which in turn is removed from man's dominion, subject as it is to unpredictable factors such as sun, wind, rain, storms, pests, predators . . .

Cyclicity, staticity (ever the same cyclical phases, in accord with human life which resembles nature in its cycle of birth, the bloom of youth and adulthood, old age, death), *passivity* and *waiting* are the classic characteristics of this type of economy and work that are most reflected in its cultural and religious categories. Trust in providence and Christian resignation in the face of misfortune for the sake of reward in heaven: these are the dominant elements on which Christian thought built its rites, doctrine and daily obligations, all centred on the family which, like a little church, became the basic cell, whose union with others formed the village (*communitas*) or church (*ecclesia*). The people of God was made up not of individuals but of *family hearths*, coming together in chapels as people met each other in the close-knit cities of the middle ages. Pastoral care, feast days, the liturgical sub-division of time and space (the sacred brought to earth), the Sunday ritual, the innumerable saints' days spread over the weeks, as though to alleviate the harshness of unending work in the fields—unless interrupted by the inclemencies of the weather; the extreme poverty of the mass of the population, most of whom lived in miserable hovels: all these influenced the religious feeling of the age.

In the medieval West, where Christianity was the only *cultural regulator*, religion tried to fulfil this role, intrinsically necessary to this way of life; this was the basis for the process of reflection that was eventually to produce the *Summae*, the admirable structure of Scholasticism, on the one hand, and on the other, the splendid manifestations of religious art—the *Domus Dei* had to be beautiful precisely because most of the houses in which people lived were squalid. The soaring spires of the cathedrals, the pealing bells, the ritual held out to sanctify every act of human life (sacramentals), came to sacralise a generally wretched way of life, attenuating its sufferings through the Christian ethic of brotherhood and love.[3] Craftsmanship was a homely occupation, the workshop being generally in the house or next to it, and structured on family lines, the mantle passing from father to sons. The joining together of craftsmen in the Guilds was the other decisive element in structuring medieval life, tied as these were to the building of churches, the religious life (*fraternitas*), particular feasts, strictly ethical codes of practice. Husbandry imbued with sacralism and craft work begetting good works were the two pillars on which medieval Christianity built its richest image of itself, an image that still shines through some of its literature, which has stood the test of passing time and changing fashion, a marvellous instrument for the expression of the Christian vision.

But the reverse side of the coin also needs examining. An agricultural life made up of weekly 'chores' was still at the mercy of the elements and events; whole peoples literally died of hunger; endless local wars led to continual spoliations; periodic revolts against poverty and suffering protested against the insecurity of life, the burden of work tying people by legal bonds to the land (glebe slaves). Epidemics were common, infant mortality high and the average expectation of life only forty years. A paternalist authoritarianism was often backed up by ecclesiastical sanctions and hardly modified by ecclesiastical benefits. Infanticide and alcoholism were rife, along with a hundred other manifestations of human suffering.

All this contradicts the image of the Middle Ages handed down as a 'Golden Age', often for ecclesiastical and religious reasons. In fact, it was a hard and difficult age in which to live for the overwhelming majority of the people. The remnants of such societies, still remembered by old people today with bitterness, show why people fled the land to work in cities whenever industry provided them with a chance to do so. It is true that theological thinking and the work of the Church served to alleviate the sufferings of the daily grind: fighting off any assault against social coherence (this is how heresy was seen); sprinkling the daily life of the *communitas* with feast days (*strong* moments); rejecting callings that seemed ill-suited to the harmonious moral development of family life; punishing usury and the gaining of riches through speculation; furnishing religious ideals (the Crusades) to the craving for war ever present in City States large and small; above all working through the example of the religious orders, in the field of work as well as that of charitable works for the good of others.[4]

In this way there developed a theology of work expressed in the key of resignation-expiation, of the 'inescapable response to the necessities of life' and of punishment for original sin. But the Christian laity were brought up in the activities of the Guilds through which almost all activities, including cultural ones, were expressed, with the sole exception of the activity of worship, which itself was financed by the Guilds themselves.

Since the theology of work was almost exclusively a '*theologia crucis*', one of suffering and discomfort, ecclesiastical practice tended to concentrate on *individual* prospects of salvation, set in the context of the continual *memento mori* so prominent in the Christian and social concept of death as the last act of meaningful importance in a life seen entirely as preparation for it. The *danse macabre* and the *ars moriendi* are excellent examples of the ecclesiastical practice of 'Christianising' popular culture. In these cases, it was the individual act that had implications for society, since a happening such as death affected everyone, subject as they were to the same eventual fate. As a matter of socio-theological observation: when life was ruled by agricultural labour and craft work, the *practices* of the Church were geared to the people of God and their daily hopes and fears, whereas *learned* (theological) thought remained disconnected from practice and characterised by references to concepts such as power and law, concerns of the nobility who lived a life of *otium* reminiscent of the ancient Greeks and Romans. Particularly in the sixteenth and seventeenth centuries, theology seemed to turn away from the existential problems of the great majority of the people, and this at a time when the moneyed and noble classes were adopting a 'georgic', rural way of life in which time spent in the city was but a brief interlude snatched from country life. This is a typical example of 'theological alienation' from current thought, perhaps brought about by the fact that most theology was made by monks, used to at most extending their own spirituality, based on flight from the world, to the laity. *The takeover of theological reflection by ecclesiastics, dating from the third and fourth centuries, with no lay intervention, went hand-in-hand with monastic appropriation of that doctrinal reflection which should (but does not) guide the greater number of those engaged in the daily round of work.*

3. THE INDUSTRIAL REVOLUTION AND THE THEOLOGY OF 'DEMIURGIC PLURALISM'

The transition from the tool to the machine marked the first industrial revolution, and from the machine-tool to the automated machine the second.[5] Both took place within the space of two hundred years and in those countries where they happened first, now highly industrialised, have completely submerged not only agriculture and the peasant economy but the whole world of values of agricultural-rural civilisation. The advent of the machine gave rise to cultural phenomena which completely upset the system of religious-ethical values and their hierarchisation. Money became the yardstick by which the success or failure of any individual or community was measured; success was displayed by means of status symbols based on wealth; the Calvinistic ethic embraced wordly success seen as a measure of divine election; production and profit, seen as goals to be achieved on earth, produced the goods and then the need for them, setting in motion the all-powerful levelling mechanism of 'consumerism' and producing the manipulated 'one-dimensional' man attacked by current philosophers and ideologies. Wealth has transformed daily life. The city has become a powerful magnet, in which most of the populations of developed countries now live, and a life-style has emerged which sociologists call 'anonymous' or 'secular'. Horizontal and vertical mobility have become both a sign of progress and an economic need, characterised by the shock produced by uprooting from one's own environment (emigration) and the lottery of success (achievement). We struggle to rise above our scholastic and functional levels to an economic model demanding continuous creativity and change (fashion) though the injection of ever new products; the mass-media project this model, imposing products created for use not by need but by hunger for profit. With the decline of a whole world based on *order* (everyone in his proper place), on fidelity to tradition, customs, the wisdom of the ancients (gerontocracy) and social control which no-one seeks to question, new cultural categories emerge, based on *mobility* as a value: ever-changing public opinion, the tyranny of fashion, libertarian permissiveness, a youth culture that follows every latest innovation, with no resistance to change. The sudden—too sudden, let us say—transition from one period to another is causing radical and deep universal crises, as evidenced by processes of role-reversal, loss of identity and upheaval of values—the two-sided phenomenon of 'being with it', destroying the world of traditional values (inconoclasm) and inventing new ones (idolatry). The disappearance of agricultural labourers and peasant culture leaves room for new forms and ways of association. Following the vision of cooperation across the boundaries of social levels (the corporation) comes the association between members of one class (the trade union); a more democratic approach is now gradually appearing in enterprises, which are modifying their structures from the model of the monastery, barracks or family to more open, dynamic and elastic ones. The family is no longer the centre of all activities, other agents replacing it in a host of ways: schools, parties, unions, peer groups, fashions. The sacred world of the individual or the group seems to centre on the three areas of orientation to the transcendent (religion), to earthly ideals (beliefs) and to indifference and pragmatism (levelling). The shorter working week, the introduction of organisational techniques (Taylor) and the assembly line (Ford), which many saw as symbols of progress, in fact mask the transition from mass to intensive exploitation, based on economic incentive and its high rate of production (piece work). Greater security of employment and higher levels of production, with health and safety regulations to limit dangers at work, seem to be new developments allied to technological progress, but against them must be set the monotony of many jobs, the effects of noise, occupational diseases, excessive dependence, the role of the family home reduced to that of a common dormitory, the different rhythms of life responding to different social stresses. The battle for a more human workplace will from now on be fought on an international level; its resolution, usually through 'pacific' but energetic means (strikes), call methods of working, international markets, prices and consumption into question.

Work is changing from day to day, but hidden or open forms of alienating subalterneity remain. The more generalised groups of labourers and wage-earners are in decline from their nineteenth-century heyday, and more specialised groups of engineers and technicians are on the increase, together with 'white collar' workers and administrative bureaucracies. The overall view of the craftsman who sees his artefact through from conception to finish is giving way to the 'partial' approach in which workers work with others—to whom they are very closely bound—in order to produce one part of a finished product, the whole of which represents the labour of hundreds of specialists and hundreds of operations. Programmed organisation of other people is not confined to the business enterprise, but extends into the leisure field, planned in relation to consumption.

Nevertheless, the world of today is one of enormous religious potential: free time, the *conscious* possibility (in common freedom) of choosing one's own creed and the type of obligation that goes with it; the decline of many of the Church's supply roles that leaves it free to concentrate on essentials; the taking over of many ecclesiastical functions previously reserved to the clergy by the laity; the growing importance of the religious community 'of intention', non-residential; new relationships between members of the Church through post-conciliar structures such as pastoral councils; the presence of strong counter-culture groups whose dynamism becomes a stimulus to new efforts of social significance: all these things, and many more, permit one to talk of a 'new kind of basic religious feeling', of which the institutional Church can and should take account.

There is a new emphasis on 'collective' evangelisation and human advancement, a collective view of faith, of morals, of worship and of final salvation. Today, all pastoral action can and must take note of the 'signs of the times' and the 'people of God', two realities related in time and space.

4. PROBLEMS OPENED UP BY 'UNITARY' THEOLOGY

If it is true that this vast upheaval in the world has made the whole of theology tremble with its talk of 'the death of God' and 'anthropological change', it is also true that more accurate and attentive investigation, particularly in relation to 'ultimate values', will show the view that a desecrating cataclysm is taking place as a result of a congenital evil in present-day society to be unduly pessimistic. What is taking place, in my view, is a '*desacralising*' process, certainly affecting the 'historical' embodiments of 'ultimate values', the cloak covering the unknowable centre, and, for the first time in recorded history, biting into the institutional theologies of the great religions; but the collective memory can reach back to other 'anthropological changes' and other 'deaths of God' which humanity has survived.[6]

Reactions to the present secularisation process and the shattering of the sacred cosmos, individual and collective, as well as to new conditions of life based largely on *having* in order to be,[7] have given rise to the tentative solutions of the new theologies—of hope, of liberation, of the third and fourth worlds—largely based on local realities (the first reacting against the tendencies of central European pessimism, the second against late capitalist models of society, the others against reformist tendencies that take no account of local traditions). With them, theological reflection on conditions of work have moved from a medieval view of 'the tribute that must be paid to original sin' and 'means to help the poor' to a more thought-out and more articulate mode—'collaboration in the work of creation', 'collaboration in redemption', brotherly aid, activities that benefit the whole family of man—reflecting the views expressed in the most recent conciliar documents and the writings of theologians such as Chenu, Rahner, Ratzinger, Pannenberg and others.

What is still called the 'theology of work' seems largely contradictory in this context, even in its most recent garb of 'theology of the workers'. This has in fact to be something more than a theological reflection on a single aspect of life, however central, composed of emblematic syntheses made by others. The need to go beyond the model of a 'compartmentalised' view of life to an overall viewpoint is a methodological one in the first place, but involves basic theological implications. This means—on the one hand—that distinctions must be made, capable of establishing 'the diversity of conditions affecting the various levels of being and having' and so of pointing to the possibility of overcoming them, once the limiting conditions of existence decline (freedom from want, from ignorance . . .). On the other hand, theology today should pay attention to what is *gradually* and continuously emerging from the grassroots, from sections of the people of God brought together through various affinities—of work, culture, residence, interests, etc. . . . Theological reflection would then be reflection on what various groups of people actually do in their continuous quest for God and dialogue with God (or in their refusal of this option) *leaving aside the possibility of generalising from this experience*, but recognising that it is and will remain 'particular'.

This will avoid the risk of attempting a normative codification (whose vertical categories are impossible today by reason of the multiplicity of specific experiences), and of assuming that a particular experience has a general application, instead of taking it as a specific witness to be compared with other witnesses in the ecclesial communion. Cultural pluralism has shattered the homogenous cosmos into different spheres (Catholicism, marxism, laicism) and broken the world of values into different 'worlds of value', in all of which the consciousness of being a Church has to be continually striven for, in the light of both the basic guidance of the ecclesiastical magisterium and the experience of the local churches, seeing unity as something made up not of *identity*, but of *analogy* and of *willed*, rather than forced *convergence*. The ecclesial experience of Christians involved in various sectors of the productive process, referred through the churches as centres of worship, and also through family and group meetings, is vital to the growth of churches that seems essential if they are to witness to unity and diversity.[8] Attention to the values of 'otherness' will build up community values, in the sense that a church will be enriched through a multiplicity of contributions rather than through the conformist monotony of equalising forces. Local creativity, in a living culture, will interact with the wider reflections of learned culture, in a synthesis that cannot but be called 'catholic'. The magisterium will still have the task of ensuring that a basic, communal view is not fragmented by partial views, which, with the force natural to small groups, tend to elevate themselves into universal visions, to impose themselves as *hegemonies*.

Homogenous solutions, provided they are not imposed manipulatively, can then become occasions for general enrichment, born of confrontation at local, diocesan, national and international level. Then, the world of work, no longer seen as the only basic aspect of man (in the marxist mould) but as one of the aspects of life, and one gradually diminishing in both time and importance,[9] can produce indications of life-styles, interests, ethical and cultural standpoints, and so indicate paths to be followed.

The overall rule to be remembered is the *transitory nature* of examples, as well as the *courage* required to try new initiatives, which can no longer be taken as lasting for all time, in the medieval manner, but perhaps only for the space of a morning. In this way we will recapture the experience of the first Christians and also that of the Exodus, which previously seemed destined to live only as historical memories. Theology should not only reflect on earthly realities, however, but, in my view, should propose *salutary reactions* to these realities, no longer allowing man to be the instrument of inanimate forces. In this sense, a *deep consciousness of current trends* is the first requirement for such theological reflection, to be followed by evaluation in the ethical field and deeper reflection on the ecclesial and practical implications.

What emerges from the above considerations is the extraordinary ambivalence of certain aspects of the reality of work. To take two examples:

(A) The real danger today (as I have often repeated) lies in the *process of homogenisation*, which as an essential component of the economic model of intensive production, tends on one hand to render the roles of the great majority of operatives conformist and bureaucratic, while on the other singling out a few of the élite (scientists, technicians, inventors) who are able to guide this highly complex technological process: so we have an amorphous mass directed by a 'select' few. This is the danger known as 'technocracy'—the dominion of a limited number of technicians over not only the manufacturing processes but over the policies that shape life-styles, social life and development. In the name of technique, *political* choices are made, on which the destiny of millions depends, choices which are obviously not limited to purely technical considerations, since they concern the world of value judgments, of objectives to be pursued and of the means that society decrees to be licit in the achievement of these objectives.[10] The morality of these choices is determined (particularly in the multi-national companies) by purely economic considerations, i.e., profit.

There are various ways of facing up to this danger, such as:

(i) Extending the concept of 'work' to embrace extra-economic activities and so breaking down the *rigidity of the role of the worker* (a subordinate role), a rigidity which today expresses a value judgment: only those who work in a particular way—manually, productively, for wages, etc.—are workers, and therefore real men. This extension of the deeper meaning of the term 'worker' enables us to give a human (and religious) response to many qualities formerly forgotten simply because of their apparent unproductiveness: poetry, prophecy, serenity, wisdom, willingness to listen to other people, devoting one's free time to others, involvement in social and civic affairs, prayer. . . . If everything of importance for collective life, and particularly everything that is definitely aimed toward the benefit of other people can be given a positive ethical valuation, then a resistance to the current overriding tendency to limit productive roles to those that are economically and biologically productive will be set up, and activities that used to be considered 'hobbies', if not written off as 'idleness' will come to be given a socially positive valuation. The revaluation of these activities will broaden the number of those who make a significant contribution to society, giving them a social reward which is at least part payment in itself for their sacrifice of time and effort. This undermines the basis of the strong antagonism currently produced by enterprises which can give enormous economic rewards because these are spread over a handful of the 'chosen few'.

(ii) Striking at the base of the current tendency to conformism and bureaucratisation produced by the type of 'replaceable' man required by the economic model of neo-capitalism and the centralised bureacracies of the socialist countries. This will undermine the mechanism that creates a privileged few (technicians, politicians, economists) self-invested with the demiurgic power not only of providing the rest with their means of livelihood but also of guiding their choices, as if they were perpetual children, and, through their control of fashion, authoritatively imposing choices in a way that keeps consumers in permanent subjection. The best response to this tendency is the offer of *equal possibilities of participation* (through a process of socialisation through education in which all take part equally), thereby stimulating the creative powers of each individual (because each individual is gifted with sufficient charisma to express himself fully) and favouring not conformity but *diversity*. In this way, and accepting not only personal diversity but that of groups (the homogeneity of cultural attachments)—any groups—he will contribute to the creation of a society made up of myriads of micro-societies, each one self-motivated, an articulated society rich in ferment, in creativity, in consciousness. This will need a theological process of reflection guiding society toward a state in which, as the old adage puts it: '*Quod tangit omnes ab omnibus adprobari debet*'. Decentralisation, plurality of experiences, multiplicity of choices, variety of ecclesial practices, should all provide theology with a challenge from which spiritual enrichment must result.

(iii) Giving an impetus to various groups of workers and to the inevitable common concerns of professional groups. In this way we can offer elements of a political counter-culture consonant with one of the main aims of the Church, to be the 'critical conscience' of humanity. Social activity at the lowest levels, inspired by a whole variety of ways of coming together as common interest groups, spontaneously, seems to provide the best chance of a solution to the current danger of 'massification'.[11]

(B) A way must be found for the 'religious' laity to produce an internal expression of the richness of their spiritual and theological reflection on the meaning of their own actions, thereby combating the tendency to invest the choices of the current economic model with an ethical valuation applied to individuals and groups, as well as the tendency for significant observations on the actions of the many to be made by a handful of experts alone—in this case professional theologians, who are almost all clerics. In this way, reflection on one's own activities in terms of ethical or even mystical valuation will come to mean conscious realisation of one's own right and duty to act in a personal (but not just individualistic) way for the common good.

Any ethical reflection on the economic motives (reward) underlying the economic model of increasing well-being for all will single out the real ethical suppositions proper to this model, and require it to become 'ethical' in itself, in the manner of the 'ethical State'. The supposition that any economic decision aimed at profit through productivity, by the mere fact of creating areas of common consent with regard to the goods produced, *thereby represents a step forward for humanity*, by virtue of the fact that well-being is a socially and ethically important good, *should be seen as a pseudo-ethical supposition of an extremely negative nature and a theological aberration 'in terminis'*. And yet there are many Christians (even including some theologians) who see nothing incongruous in the statements that: (*a*) well-being is an ethically positive thing regardless of the social cost it entails; (*b*) the *economic benefit* itself considered necessary for the creation of wealth should be divorced from the 'means' by which this is produced and generalised.

The short-sighted reasoning behind so much of the ecological destruction at present being carried out derives partly, it is true, from lack of social imagination, but also from lack of theological reflection on the social relevance of decisions that are only apparently of individual or technical concern. Critical reflection on the aims, latent or open, of the current economic model, on its way of achieving its aims, its technical, monetary and consumerist trappings, on the huge fortunes it creates for a minority (at the expense of the majority), could shed some light on practices that seem orientated to the good of society but in fact are based on decisions taken on totally 'élitist' political grounds and adversely affecting the majority.

Here, as with other 'burning' issues of the day, theology must abandon its neutral stance and learn to intervene critically on behalf of mankind by clarifying the issues so that a so-called short-term advantage (increasing levels of well-being) does not in fact produce immediate and irreparable damage to everyone. It also needs saying that a dispassionate examination of the limitations of present-day theology as applied to the problems of work, the conduct of business, economic programming and the general interests of workers, shows up the *basic irrelevance* of most ethical and political reflection on these matters. Problems such as *security of work* (in all senses); the permissibility of decisions involving *exploitation* of social groups or regions, or of energy and natural resources, with no social concern either short- or long-term; a so-called 'business morality' which in practice seems to justify the maxim 'business is business'; the legality of enterprises *dedicated solely to speculation* through playing the stock market and similar pursuits; the *economy of plunder* at the expense of developing countries; not to mention questions such as ecological choices, alternative sources of energy, mobility of labour—all these are chapter headings for a theology that needs serious study, as political theology rather than as moral theology or a theology of work.[12] And it is not by chance that decisions of this kind and of such importance lead to basic consideration of the meaning of the type of life chosen: whether it favours quantity or quality; whether it is ethnocentric (even if this applies only to highly industrialised countries) or polycentric; how much it respects the rights and freedoms of others; if—finally—it tends to combat 'false needs' or to create them.

As a last word, it might be useful to point out that in the final analysis, charity, always more personalised on the fringes of society, demands a basic Christian choice involving the reinstatement—not as a marginal element imposed by circumstances, but as a 'central value'—of the option for sacrifice and austerity which the Christian world seems to have forgotten, blinded as it is by the glow of the false dawn of technological progress, passed off as a full expression of human and spiritual development.

Translated by Paul Burns

Notes

1. General information on the nomadic life can be found in A. Keit *The Antiquity of Man* (London 1925); J. Koty *Die Behandlung der Alten und Kranken bei der Naturvölken* (Stuttgart 1931); A. C. Blanch *Origine e Sviluppo dei popoli cacciatori e raccogliatori* (Rome 1956); J. Pfeiffez *The Emergence of Man* (London 1971); C. D. Darlington *The Evolution of Man and Society* (London 1969); S. L. Washburn *Social Life of Early Man* (Chicago 1961).

2. On patriarchal agricultural families, see the important contributions by Dudy, Hanck, Klapisch, Payen, Tenenti and others in *Famille et parenté dans l'occident mediéval* (Rome 1977) and that of by P. Aries in *L'enfant et la vie familiale sous l'ancienne régime* (Paris 1960).

3. On the allegedly deep religiosity of the middle ages, so praised by Huizinga, it is possible to have serious doubts. See the contributions of G. Le Bras in *Etudes de sociologie religieuse* 2 Vols (Paris 1952-6).

4. On this point there is the important work by J. Le Goff *Tempo della chiesa e tempo del mercante* (Milan 1977); also T. Noonan *The Scholastic Analysis of Usury* (New York 1957).

5. I am indebted to G. Lefranc *Histoire du travail et des travailleurs* (Paris 1975); C. Fohlen *Le Travail aux XIXe siècle* (Paris 1967); various *Il problema della società industriale* (Milan 1979).

6. This is a theory of mine developed in *Uno spiraglio sul futuro* (Pisa 1974). Based on intuitions of the anthropologist Gehlen, it envisages new ways of life which will enable modern man to grow in religious stature in comparison with his past, though this is influential.

7. E. Fromm *To Have or To Be* (New York 1976).

8. I have treated this subject more fully in 'L'uguale e il diverso' *Sicurezza sociale* 3 (1978) 571-605.

9. Recent researches in France point to the likelihood of a drastic reduction of labour in the near future, since the advent of automation and new technologies will seriously curtail requirements for productive man-power. This raises two important questions: Who will the privileged few be who control the means of production? What will the rest do? A European policy of reducing working hours seems an inescapable need, as does a policy of restructuring life-styles so as to leave little time for subordinate or executive work and a lot for a new kind of free time, born of the impossibility of work for everyone.

10. In this case, technique is clearly not operating autonomously but as a function of capital. See A. Ure *La filosofia delle manifatture* (Turin 1863), p. 98; L. Gilkey *Il destino della Religione nell'era tecnologica* (Rome 1972).

11. This observation does not apply to corporate organisations, but to confrontations/meetings between various parties, of a non-violent and non-mandatory nature.

12. In my view, theology does not possess a sufficient framework of certainty to allow of its automatic application to every social situation. Critical reflection on what is happening, the basic role of the laity, the contribution of various social components, all help to establish the method of continuous criticism through which points that seemed to have been definitively established are once again called into question.

Rudolf Siebert

Work and Religion in Hegel's Thought

THE aim of this study is to explore critically Georg W. F. Hegel's philosophy and theology of work.[1] Hegel was the first powerful thinker of the modern West expressively to make labour the subject matter of philosophical discourse.[2] He was the first modern philosopher, who reflected in principle on what work as well as religion mean for man's self-formation, humanisation and emancipation. Hegel thought about the relation between labour and religion at the beginning of capitalist industrialisation in civil society, when the business cycle started and the first economic depression made manifest not only the positive, benevolent, but also the negative, malignant, tragic dialectic of work.[3]

Without Hegel's philosophy of work and religion the modern discovery of the connection between labour and human consciousness would have been unlikely. Only out of and against Hegel's theological philosophy of work, Karl Marx and Max Weber could develop their own theories of labour and religion. When today critical theorists or positivists study the correlation between religion and working class or petite bourgeoisie, they do so not only against the Hegelian theory of work and religion but also on the basis of its accomplishments. At present a critical theological reflection on work and religion would remain deficient without reference to Hegel's fundamental and lasting achievements. We will explore Hegel's thought on work and religion in critical discourse with the contemporary Hegelian Jürgen Habermas's dialectical theory of instrumental and communicative action.[4] Like no other thinker in recent decades, Habermas has demonstrated the actuality of Hegel's theory of work and religion for advanced capitalist and socialist society, even in points in which he must oppose Hegel sharply on grounds of his own materialistic presuppositions.

1. LIBERATION

In 1803 Hegel wrote an essay *On the Scientific Treatment of Natural Law* and begun to lecture on the *System of Social Morality* at the University of Jena, Germany.[5] Here Hegel offers a distinctive basis for the self-formation process of the human spirit. Hegel discusses four dialectical patterns: work, marital and familial love, language and the struggle for recognition. Man liberates himself through these four dialectical dimensions. Each sphere mediates in its own specific way between subject and object, man and his world. The dialectic of labour is fundamental for man's liberation. The dialectical unity of all four potentialities of human freedom renders the structure of man's self-consciousness transparent. We concentrate on the dialectic of work and how it pushes beyond itself not only into the dialectic of love, language and communicative praxis, but also into the religious and theological dimension.[6]

2. MORAL TOTALITY

From the very beginning in the essay on natural law, Hegel discusses work and religion in the context of the moral totality.[7] It includes the spheres of work as well as of familial love, language and recognition. Concretely it is the state. Needs, work, possessions and enjoyment occur continually in the moral totality. In their infinite entanglements and complications, needs, work, possessions and enjoyment are under the law of external necessity. They constitute a system of universal dependence inside the moral totality as system of freedom, besides the dimensions of marital love, symbolic representation and communicative action. The system of needs, work, possessions and enjoyment as science is the political economy. Throughout his life Hegel is deeply involved in political economy and admires it.[8]

Inside the moral totality the system of dependence or of reality is completely immersed in negativity and bad infinity. There is no end to needs, work, possessions and enjoyment. Therefore the moral totality must treat the system of dependence entirely negatively. Only the negation of the negation leads to concrete human freedom. What by its very nature is negative, the system of reality, must remain something negative. It must not be allowed to harden itself. It must be kept in flux. Otherwise it becomes something like a 'state in the state' and as such rends asunder the moral totality. The state must control the economy.

3. DESIRE, LABOUR, ENJOYMENT

According to Hegel the system of dependence as integral part of the moral totality consists first of all in the liquidation of the original unconscious unity of nature and spirit.[9] This separation as felt by man is need. Furthermore, the system of reality is constituted by the annihilation of the separation between nature and spirit. Labour negates desire. Finally the system of reality consists in the liquidation of the object of desire as well as of work. It brings about the identity of need and work. This is the worker's enjoyment of the fruits of his labour.

In Hegel's view the feeling of the individual involved in the system of dependence is in the form of the difference between spirit and nature, subject and object, desire and enjoyment. Hegel comprehends this feeling of the individual in the system of reality as a differentiated totality in itself. This totality exists as negative practical perception, i.e., as labour, as product and possession, as a tool. Of the three moments the tool is the most important element in the differentiated totality of the worker's feeling.

4. TOOL

For Hegel the importance of the tool lies in its centre position between the subject and his or her desire on one hand and the objects.[10] The tool is torn away from nature. It does no longer belong to nature as does, e.g., the child, which constitutes the centre in the dialectic of sexual love.[11] On one hand the tool is subjective. The tool is the power of the working subject. It is completely determined by the worker. It is prepared and worked over by the labourer. On the other hand, the tool is objectively directed against the thing which is the material of the working process. Through the tool as centre, the subject supersedes the immediacy of his or her own destruction. In itself the working process is not only the liquidation of the object, but also of the subject. It is the negation of the worker. The subject is totally quantified in the labour process. Hand and spirit of the worker become obtuse, dull and apathetic. They assume themselves the nature of the negative and the formless. This is the negative dialectic of labour.

The tool of work as the middle between the worker and the world of objects is the real rationality of the labour process. In the tool the worker separates from himself or herself the dullness of work. The worker gives something else, something inorganic up to the destructive power of the working process. The subject imposes on another the subjective part of the negativity of work. At the same time through the tool, the work of the subject ceases to be something entirely singular. In the instrument of work the subjectivity of the worker has been elevated to universality. In principle everybody can imitate the instrument—the plough, the hammer, the screwdriver, etc. Everybody can work with the tool like everybody else. This way the tool is the continual and universal rule of work. That is the positive dialectic of work.

Because of its rationality, the tool as centre between subject and object stands higher than the working process and higher than the object worked on for the enjoyment and higher than the enjoyment as the purpose of work. Therefore all primitive, archaic and historical-intermediate nations, as far as they still stand in the potentiality of nature, have honoured greatly the instrument of labour. Hegel finds this respect for the tool as well as the awareness of it most beautifully expressed in Homer's epic. There seems to be something sacred in the tool. It has a theological core. Only in modernity, in the process of capitalist and socialist industrialisation, the tool loses its aura and becomes profane.

In any case, the tool, in which the labourer's experience of the world of objects is deposited, constitutes not only universality but also permanence against the ephemeral and fleeting moments of desire and enjoyment. It alone remains, when the worker and the object he works on, are long gone. The instrument is inherited from one generation to the other, while the subject who desires and the object which is desired, only subsist as individuals and in their singularity continually pass away. There is something 'eternal' about the tool of work.

5. MASTER AND SERVANT

Hegel sees work in the context of the relationship of lordship and bondage in his Jena lectures on the system of morality as well as four years later in his *Phenomenology of Mind*.[12] According to Hegel, through work the worker's consciousness comes home to itself. The worker finds his singular identity through his work. The desire of the master has reserved to itself the pure negating of the object in enjoyment. Thereby the master keeps an unalloyed, unbroken feeling of himself. But the satisfaction of the master is precisely for that reason itself only a state of evanescence. It lacks objectivity, universality, rationality, subsistence. The labour of the worker on the other hand is desire restrained and checked. Transitoriness is delayed. The work of the labourer shapes the thing. The worker's negative relation to the thing passes into its form. It moves into something that is permanent. The negative activity of the worker giving shape and form to the object produces at the same time the pure self-existence of his consciousness. In the work of the worker, his consciousness is externalised, objectivised and reified and thus passes into the condition of permanence. The worker's consciousness as it toils and serves accordingly attains by this means the direct apprehension of that independent being, as itself. So the labourer finds his personal identity through the thing, which he has produced. While his master becomes the victim of the negative dialectic of work, losing his identity, the worker becomes the usufructuary of the positive dialectic of labour, achieving his identity. In a very long and often very tragic process the dialectic of master and servant leads over the freedom of the One and the Few to the freedom of All. Here freedom is not understood as bourgeois arbitrariness, but as a person's identity with himself or herself in solidarity with the others.

6. GOD'S SPIRIT

As Hegel proceeds in his description of the dialectic of work from the original absolute unity of nature and spirit, this presupposition shapes greatly his concept of the unity of man's formative process, his self-emancipation in the diverse dimensions of work, love, language and recognition.[13] In Hegel's view, in nature spirit has its complete external objectivity. Spirit therefore finds its identity in the sublation of this externalisation not only in work, but also in marital love, linguistic competence and communicative praxis. Spirit thus is the absolute presupposition of nature to dialectical thought, Spirit, which first of all appears as the consequence and evolutionary product of nature, reveals itself as being the absolute prius of nature through which it seems to be mediated.[14]

From the very beginning in the Jena essay on natural law and the system of social morality Hegel comprehends theologically the dialectic of work, as well as the dialectic of the love of the sexes, of symbolic representation and of the struggle for dominion. The truth of nature is incorporated in the tool of the worker. The innermost centre of nature is spirit.[15] Nature only becomes comprehensible in its essence and comes to itself in man's confrontation with it in the dialectic of work as well as of love, language and recognition. The spiritual interior of nature is expressed in the universal and rational rules, incorporated in the tools of the worker, who is working on nature. Hidden subjectivity can always be found in what has been objectivised. Behind the mask of objects, nature can always be revealed as the concealed opponent. Therefore, the basic dialectical dimension of work can be reduced to one common denominator with the dialectic of the struggle for dominion. The relationship of the worker to nature can be brought within the configuration of reciprocal recognition. The intersubjectivity in which one self-consciousness can identify with another self-consciousness without relinquishing the non-identity between itself and the other is established in labour when the object confronting the working individual is from the outset conceived theologically as an opposite with which interaction in the mode of that between subjects is possible.

According to Hegel the dialectic of recognising oneself in the other is bound to the relationship of communicative interaction between subjects who are in principle equal. As soon as nature in its totality is elevated to a subject in opposition to the united subjects of work, as indeed it happens in the transition from nature religions to religions of spiritual subjectivity and to the religion of truth and freedom—Christianity—this relation of parity no longer holds.[16] There cannot be any longer a dialogue between spirit and nature and a struggle for recognition which results in a constituted moral relationship of equal partners. The God's spirit is solitary in Judaism, Islam and bourgeois Deism.

The unity of God's spirit with itself and with a nature, from which it differentiates itself as its other, can at the end of history of religions in Christianity, no longer be conceived of in terms of the pattern of the intersubjectivity of working, loving, speaking and mutually recognising individuals. The dialectical unity of spirit and nature in which spirit does not recognise itself in nature as an antagonistic subject, but only finds itself as in a counterpart, can more readily be constructed from the experience of the self-reflection of consciousness. Therefore Hegel conceives of the movement of God's spirit in terms of the model of self-reflection. Hegel renews the neoplatonic and thomistic idea of the exitus-reditus-circulatio structure of God's spirit: From God through the world as nature and history to God.[17]

Hegel is fully aware of the fact that the modern problem of the difference, the relative autonomy and unity of the fundamental dimensions of human emancipation—work, love, language and recognition—cannot be resolved unless the absolute identity of the subject with the whole of nature is rendered comprehensible.[18] What Hegel wants to make intelligible to modern people is that the world of nature and the world of history are held together by a unifying power which, in the process of unfolding itself, produces these diremptions between nature and man as well as among the spheres of physical and intellectual work, marital and familial love, symbolic representation and communicative praxis, but can at the same time again conquer these dichotomies. For Hegel this power is God's spirit as love, which unites what is separated.

Hegel has undertaken the attempt of producing for modern consciousness a system of knowledge guaranteeing identity through the dialectics of work, love, language and recognition in a similar way as once the nature religions—Taoism, Hinduism, Buddhism—and the religions of subjectivity—Zoroastrianism, Syrian, Egyptian, Roman, Greek and Jewish religion—did for archaic and historic-intermediate consciousness, but now under the conditions of Christianity and of the subjective freedom initiated by it.[19] In principle Hegel is able in civil society to locate the dialectics of work, love, language and recognition within God's *exitus-reditus-circulatio* process of self-mediation. Thus each dialectical medium can illuminate the point at which the modern subject finds his or her place in God's history. The dynamic structure of God's spirit which renders comprehensible both nature and history as well as the spheres of labour, love, language and recognition in their essential manifoldness and unity is at the same time the structure in which the modern individual can find and preserve his or her singular personal identity. For Hegel to render comprehensible means concretely: to eradicate all contingencies—injustice, sickness, death—which threaten the personal identity of subjects and the particular identity of nations. It is through the very acts of comprehension that the subject identifies himself or herself with God's absolute spirit which in itself produces the annihilation of what is night and nothing and renders futile that which is futile in terms of the negation of the negation present in all mediations of human freedom, particularly in the dialectic of work.

For Hegel the universal *exitus-reditus-circulatio* movement of God's spirit is made intelligible by the dialectical mediations of labour, love, linguistic competence and struggle for dominion, not withstanding their particularity in that they are embodiments and the realisation of man's humanisation and liberation. Modern society finds whatever singular and particular identity it has in the dimensions of work, love, language and recognition in so far as they are rooted in the universal identity of God's spirit and love. According to Hegel, it is the task of a theological philosophy to show this fourfold identity of man in work, love, speech acts and communicative action to be rational and thereby to overcome a merely lukewarm approximation to the truth and more so still the cold desperation concerning the persisting misery the world is in.

7. SACRIFICE

For Hegel the power of sacrifice consists in the perceiving and objectivising of man's involvement with inorganic reality.[21] Sacrifice is work and work is sacrifice. For Hegel all religious work is cultic work and all cultic work, from the bodily movement of dancing to the construction of huge temples, falls into the sphere of sacrifice. In the case of the sacrifice the purpose is the universality of the God against which the individual subjects must give themselves up in action. Religious work is in general a giving up not only of external things but, as the history of religions progresses, also of man's own internal subjectivity.

In Hegel's view cult as sacrifice starts from the presupposition of an original unity between man and God. But often deviations occur from this original identity. Deflections happen from this original reconciliation or from a lack of a need for it. This non-identity can be caused by the arbitrariness of the individual, captive of the enjoyments and pleasures of the world, or by the power of nature, by misfortunes of individuals and nations. After such disturbances of the original unity between God and man, e.g., sickness, death, war, injustices, floods, fires, earthquakes, serious negation, hard religious work, great sacrifices are necessary in order to restore again the original identity. In this case of tragic, painful non-identity between the divine and the human the meaning of cult as sacrificial work is not to enjoy their original unity but rather to liquidate their present disunion. But even in this case there is still the presupposition of the original reconciliation in and for itself without which the negation of the present non-identity through hard sacrificial religious work could not be successful.

But in the last analysis for Hegel it is not only man who sacrifices things or himself in religious work in order to overcome diremptions in the moral totality. God himself sacrifices himself.[22] God himself eternally gives birth to himself in the objectivity of nature and history and in this his character of objectivity surrenders himself to suffering and death and from its ashes ascends to glory. The Divine in its shape and objectivity, has an immediately dual nature. Not only man, but God himself engages in sacrificial work in the huge slaughterhouse and on the golgatha of the world as nature and history. Hegel's concept of God, sacrifice and work is emphatically Christological.

8. FORCES OF PRODUCTION

Hegel's great disciple and opponent, Marx, without any knowledge of the latter's essay on the natural law and the lectures on the system of social morality, rediscovered nevertheless on his own the dialectical interconnection between labour on one hand and communicative action, love and language on the other hand in the dialectic between the forces of production and the productive relations.[23] In a critique of the last chapter of Hegel's *Phenomenology of the Spirit*, on absolute knowledge of the absolute, Marx maintained that Hegel had, indeed, taken the viewpoint of modern political economy.[24] He had comprehended labour as the very essence of man, in which man has confirmed himself. In his Paris manuscript on political economy and philosophy, Marx finds the greatness of Hegel's phenomenology and its final result in the fact that he comprehends, indeed, the self-generation of man as a process, the objectivisation as the process of confronting objects, as externalisation and as sublation of this externalisation and that he thus comprehends the essence of labour and conceives objective man, the true, because the actual, man, as the result of his own labour.[25]

From this point of view Marx himself, like Hegel before, attempted to reconstruct the world-historical process by which individuals, nations and the human species form, humanise and emancipate themselves in terms of the laws of the reproduction of social life by work. However, Habermas's correct analysis of the first part of Marx's *German Ideology* reveals that Marx does not actually explicate the dialectical relationship between labour on one side and communicative action, familial love, and language on the other side as Hegel had been able to do on theological grounds.[26] Marx instead, under the unspecific title of social praxis reduces communicative action as well as marital love and language to instrumental action. Just as in Hegel's system of social morality the use of tools mediates between subject and object so for Marx instrumental action, the productive activity which regulates the metabolism between the human species and its natural environment becomes the paradigm for the generation of all four dimensions of human liberation. While according to Hegel the self-movement of God's absolute spirit is the foundation for the differentiation and convergence of work, love, language and recognition, for Marx, who declares Hegel's God concept to be mere bourgeois ideology, i.e., false consciousness, all four dimensions are resolved into the self-movement of material production.[27] Because of this reductionism, due to a scientistic misreading of Hegel's theology, Marx's brilliant insight into the dialectical relationship between the forces of production, i.e., labour, and the productive relations, i.e., family, language, political communication, could very easily be misinterpreted in a mechanistic and positivistic manner. Without theology positivism is unavoidable.[28]

9. ALTERNATIVE FUTURES

At present, when in organised capitalist and socialist societies, positivists make the attempt to reorganise the dimensions of work, family, language and communicative praxis, no matter how much they may have hardened in advanced modernity, according to the model of technically progressive cybernetic systems of rational goal-directed actions, critical theorists as well as Christians have reason enough to keep the four dialectical dimensions of human liberation more rigorously separated.[29] Such separation may contain the only hope for a successful resistance against or at least mitigation of alternative Future I—the totally administered one-dimensional, technocratic society, in which instrumental action completely integrates into itself work, love, language and communicative praxis.[30]

Positivists are producing innumerable models of the future, which adhere to the idea of the progressive rationalisation of labour.[31] They intend to exclude the negative dialectic of work. Although hunger still holds sway over two-thirds of the world's population, the abolition of hunger is not an abstract Utopia. The entirely administered society could definitely increase material justice. But to set free the technical forces of production is not identical with the development of values and norms, which could fulfil the dialectic of labour, love, language and communicative action. Liberation from hunger and misery does not necessarily converge with emancipation from the spiritlessness of mechanised labour, from patriarchal distortions of marriage and family, from language regulation and servitude and degradation. More material justice must not be paid for by the loss of freedom and dignity.

There is certainly no automatic developmental relation between work on the one hand and love, language, and communicative practice on the other hand. But there is nevertheless a real connection between the four spheres of human emancipation. Hegel can persuade us of the relevance of this inter-relationship: the further self-formative process of the human spirit—individuals, nations and the species—depends on the differentiation as well as the reunion of the dialectical dimensions of work, love, language and recognition. Hegel has also clarified, where can be found, the motivation to work for the particularisation as well as universalisation of the four potentialities of human freedom, in God's infinite spirit, freedom and love. Such religious motivation can help us not only at least to mitigate alternative Future I—the totally cybernatically controlled society, and to resist unconditionally alternative Future II—new world wars, but also to prepare the way for alternative Future III—the rational and free peace society, characterised by the separation as well as by the reconciliation of work, familial love, language and solidary praxis.[32]

Notes

1. G. W. F. Hegel *Jenaer Schriften* (Berlin 1972) pp. 383-437, 444-445, 492; G. W. F. Hegel *Phänomenologie des Geistes* (Stuttgart-Bad Cannstatt 1964) pp. 156-157, 602-620; G. W. F. Hegel *Grundlinien der Philosophie des Rechts* (Stuttgart-Bad Cannstatt 1964) pp. 270, 276-278, 397, 398; G. W. F. Hegel *System der Philosophie* (Stuttgart-Bad Canstatt 1965) p. 401; G. W. F. Hegel *Verlesungen uber die Philosophie der Geschichte* (Stuttgart 1961) pp. 50-51; G. W. F. Hegel *Vorlesungen über die Philosophie der Religion* (Stuttgart-Bad Cannstatt 1965) I pp. 248-249; G. W. F. Hegel *Vorlesungen über die Philosophie der Religion* (Stuttgart-Bad Cannstatt 1965) II p. 267.

2. H. Weinstock *Arbeit und Bildung. Die Rolle der Arbeit im Prozess um unsere Menschwerdung* (Heidelberg 1969) chap. 2.

3. SW 7 pp. 270-286, 311-328; Weinstock *Arbeit* pp. 37-40, 42-44, 47-50.

4. J. Habermas *Technik und Wissenschaft als 'Ideologie'* (Frankfurt a.M. 1976) pp. 9-47; J. Habermas *Theory and Practice* (Boston) chap. 4; J. Habermas *Zur Rekonstruktion des Historischen Materialismus* (Frankfurt a.M.) chap. 4, esp. pp. 10-105.

5. Hegel *Jenaer Schriften* chaps. 5, 6; Habermas *Technik* pp. 9-10.

6. Hegel *Jenaer Schriften* pp. 383, 395-396; SW 15 pp. 248-249; SW 16 pp. 266-267; Habermas *Technik* pp. 39-44; Habermas *Zur Rekonstruktion* pp. 103-105; Weinstock *Arbeit* pp. 39, 40, 42.

7. Hegel *Jenaer Schriften* pp. 383-384.

8. *Ibid*; SW 7 pp. 270-271; R. J. Siebert *Hegel's Philosophy of History: Theological, Humanistic and Scientific Elements* (Washington, D.C. 1979) chap. 4.

9. Hegel *Jenaer Schriften* pp. 434-437; Habermas *Technik* pp. 26-27.

10. Hegel *Jenaer Schriften* pp. 444-446; Habermas *Technik* pp. 25-27.

11. R. J. Siebert *Hegel's Concept of Marriage and Family: The Origin of Subjective Freedom* (Washington, D.C. 1979) chaps. 9, 13, 15, 16.

12. Hegel *Jenaer Schriften* pp. 458-461; SW 2 pp. 156-158; SW 11 pp. 44-47; Habermas *Technik* pp. 35-37.

13. Hegel *Jenaer Schriften* pp. 395-396, 464-520, 431-463; SW 15 pp. 279-306, 324-342, 417-422; SW 16 pp. 191-209; Habermas *Technik* pp. 37-44; Habermas *Zur Rekonstruktion* pp. 10-105.

14. G. W. F. Hegel *Enzyklopädie der Philosophischen Wissenschaften* (Hamburg 1959) p. 432.

15. SW 16 p. 354.

16. SW 15 pp. 417-422; SW 16 pp. 191-209.

17. Siebert *Hegel's Philosophy* pp. 9-10; M. Seckler *Das Heil in der Geschichte* (Munchen 1964) pp. 19-132; H. Kung *Menschwerdung Göttes* (Freiburg 1970) pp. 522-557.

18. Hegel *Enzyklopädie* pp. 9-10, 45-46, 61-62, 73-74, 86-88, 95-97, 341-343, 446-448, 451-457: 63-64, 74-76, 95-96, 99-100, 171-173; SW 15 pp. 19-22, 104-114; SW 16 pp. 209-247, 354; Habermas *Zur Rekonstruktion* pp. 103-105; Habermas *Technik* pp. 39-42; Siebert *Hegel's Philosophy* II.

19. SW 15 pp. 342-472; SW 16 pp. 46-188, 191-223; Siebert *Hegel's Concept*

chaps. 1, 3, 18; R. J. Siebert *Horkheimer's Critical Sociology of Religion: The Relative and the Transcendent* (Washington, D.C. 1979) chap. VII.

20. SW 7 p. 36.

21. SW 15 pp. 248-249; Hegel *Jenaer Schriften* pp. 395-396, 519-520; Habermas *Technik* pp. 40-42.

22. Hegel *Jenaer Schriften* pp. 395-396; SW 16 pp. 295-308; SW 11 pp. 39-43, 47-50, 568-569; G. W. F. Hegel *The Phenomenology of Mind* (New York 1967) p. 64; Kung *Menschwerdung* pp. 622-631.

23. K. Marx *Die Fruhschriften* (Stuttgart 1955) chaps. 6, 7; Habermas *Technik* pp. 44-47.

24. SW 2 pp. 602-620; Marx *Fruhschriften* pp. 270-288.

25. Marx *Die Fruhschriften* pp. 269.

26. Habermas *Technik* pp. 44-47; Marx *Fruhschriften* chap. 8.

27. R. Niebuhr *Marx and Engels on Religion* (New York 1964) pp. 41-42, 69-72, 73-81.

28. M. Horkheimer *Die Sehnsucht nach dem ganz Anderen* (Hamburg 1970) pp. 54, 59-61, 86-89; M. Horkheimer *Notizen 1950 bis 1969 und Dammerung* (Frankfurt a.M. 1974) pp. 101-104, 116-117.

29. Habermas *Technik* pp. 46-47; Horkheimer *Die Sehnsucht* pp. 85-89; Horkheimer *Notizen* pp. 116-117.

30. H. Marcuse *One-Dimensional Man* (Boston 1964) chaps. 1-4; E. Fromm *The Revolution of Hope* (New York 1968) chap. 3.

31. Habermas *Technik* p. 47.

32. J. B. Metz *Theology of the World* (New York 1973) chap. 6; J. B. Metz *Glaube in Geschichte und Gesellschaft* (Mainz 1977) pp. 204-211; R. J. Siebert 'Peukert's New Critical Theology I' in *The Ecumenist* (May-June 1978) 52-58; R. J. Siebert 'Peukert's New Critical Theology II' in *The Ecumenist* (July-August 1978) 78-80.

Lee Cormie

Work and Salvation

IN THE United States the rates of separation and divorce, child abuse, suicide, homicide, admission to state mental hospitals and prisons, death from cirrhosis of the liver, heart and kidney diseases skyrocket among unemployed persons. Similarly, those rates are generally much higher among lower income people than they are among those with higher incomes. Clearly, the work we do, or don't do, profoundly affects our lives, and our deaths.

It largely determines our standard of living. It shapes our views of ourselves and others, our values and goals. And struggles over the organisation of work are key factors shaping the whole social order. For these reasons, interpretations of work inevitably involve interpretations of human nature and of the whole social order.

1. CAPITALISM PROMISES HUMANISATION

Historically, capitalism has been interpreted in terms of the division of labour which it promotes. Its supporters, like Adam Smith in his *Wealth of Nations* (1776), celebrated the virtues of this division of labour. By simplifying tasks, he thought, it speeded up production and the invention of new machines. These developments, he claimed, were responsible for the great increases in wealth in England, France and Poland in the eighteenth century.

Yet Smith was also very blunt about the costs of this division of labour. 'The understandings of the greater part of men', he wrote, 'are necessarily formed by their ordinary employments.' And because the majority of people perform tasks so simple that they require little understanding or imagination, they generally become 'as stupid and ignorant as it is possible for a human creature to become'.[1]

Smith was strangely silent about these costs. Apparently he thought that they were more than outweighed by the new wealth the system was producing. Subsequent generations of apologists for capitalism, however, have not been able to avoid these questions, and inevitably their explanations of the benefits of this division of labour have involved them in far-reaching claims about human nature, the nature of society, and the direction of history.[2] In the twenty-five-year period following World War II these claims amounted to nothing less than secularised salvation histories. Because the U.S. was widely recognised as the most 'advanced' among the developed countries, and because so many of the influential theories in this period emerged in the U.S., it will be helpful to examine these developments in the U.S. and the interpretations of them. The issue of the relevance of these claims for other countries will be examined below.

The claims are familiar ones. The logic of economic development has led to the rapid expansion of production of services, in government, education, research, etc. These developments are promoting a more highly educated and better paid work force. At the same time, advanced technology is eliminating much dull and dangerous work. The result of this 'second industrial revolution' is the increasing homogenisation of 'middle-class' American society; the working class, in this view, is literally disappearing.

The analyses of these social scientists verge on theology at precisely the point where they begin to describe the shifts in consciousness and values which correspond to the changing nature of work. Recognising that occupational experience helps to structure our views not only of the occupational world but of social reality in general,[3] they insist that the very structure of middle-class work promotes values which are both the epitome of the historical development of moral sensibilities, and the moral glue which holds together advanced capitalist societies. This kind of work is characterised by freedom from close supervision, substantially complex work, a non-routinised flow of tasks, and the need to co-operate with others. And thus it promotes in middle-class workers: the capacity and willingness to act independently, sensitivity to one's own and others' internal dynamics as well as to the external consequences of actions, open-mindedness, trustfulness of others, personal moral standards.[4]

Not surprisingly, in this view, working-class jobs promote quite different values. For the essence of these jobs is the experience of being at the mercy of forces beyond one's control, perhaps beyond one's understanding; these jobs are simple, routinised, and closely supervised, leaving little room for self-development, the exercise of initiative, or the growth of inter-personal sensitivity. The structures of these jobs, then, promote obedience to the letter of the law and to the dictates of authority, attention to the external consequences of action rather than to intentions, intolerance of non-conformity, and distrust of others.[5]

These different sets of values make sense in the lives of those who hold them precisely because they reflect the experiences and demands of everyday life as it is structured in the workplace. Inevitably these experiences colour other aspects of life, too, child-rearing practices, for example, because parents are preparing their children for futures like their own. What is at stake, then, in the claims about post-industrial society becomes clear: capitalism itself is saving us from the ravages of capitalism.

Of course, these developments are most evident in the U.S., Western Europe, and Japan. But, it was claimed, other nations will also enjoy their fruits of capitalist economic developments if they follow appropriate policies.[6]

These theories of development have much in common with traditional theological claims about meaning in life. As they picture development both in the First World and in the Third World, they parallel traditional Christian expectations of the Second Coming of Christ. Yet there is one significant difference, for the striking thing about these theories is that the *eschaton* is collapsed into the present; there is no future perfect society against which to judge the present. Salvation in many of its dimensions has been achieved.[7]

The claims of these secular salvation histories have influenced the development of theology, too. These tendencies are especially clear in the theology of work. Like so much other theology, the theologies of work which were prominent in the U.S. at this time came from Europe. There were two themes which were prominent in these theologies.[8] On the one hand, work was glorified as itself sacramental, nothing less than the externalisation and effecting of the role of Christ the King.[9] On the other hand, leisure time, i.e., time outside of work, was celebrated.[10] The first of these views idealises work; at best the characteristics of this kind of work appear only in middle-class work in the modern world. And the second draws on the distinction between work and leisure which is a product of capitalism, it seems to assume at least a benevolent work experience, not the alienating impact of working-class work. Since people no longer need to work so long or so hard to provide the necessities of life, and even some luxuries, they can give more time to intellectual, cultural and religious pursuits. In this view, these intrinsically rewarding activities, so unlike work (at least working-class work), are seen as manifestations of essential human nature.

2. CAPITALISM FALLS BELOW EXPECTATIONS

The problem with the developmentalist perspective, this secular salvation history, is that it is wrong, at least from the point of view of the majority of people in the world. When years of heroic efforts to accomplish development resulted in a better life for only an élite few, activists and scholars in the Third World, and some in the First World sympathetic to them, began to question these theories and policies. In place of these theories which picture development within each nation as naturally evolving toward the values and structures of societies like the U.S., a world system perspective is emerging which interprets the development or underdevelopment of different groups of people at different places and times in terms of the changing configuration of a single world capitalist economy.[11] The driving force of this ever-expanding system is understood to be the dialectic between corporate capital's need to expand and the efforts of different groups to resist or to transform in their interests these different strategies of capital accumulation; a key arena for these struggles is the State, because of its role in promoting the interests of its own corporations abroad, and in channelling the social surplus and maintaining social order at home.

In this view, capitalism has been a world economy since its origins in Europe in the sixteenth century; but, of course, not all parts of the system or dimensions of life within it have been affected in the same way, in the same degree, or at the same time as the others. The precise nature and degree of this impact are matters for empirical investigation. In general, however, it can be pointed out that Third World nations were incorporated into this world-wide division of labour as suppliers of slaves and raw materials. This means that from the beginning, their development has been eneven, more a response to the needs of foreign investors, and of their own internal classes in collusion with them, than to the needs of the majority of people. The structures of the world system have changed profoundly with the success of the struggles for independence; nevertheless, except for nations which, like Cuba, have attempted to withdraw from the system, the contemporary world economy continues to promote uneven development. This means that islands of substantial economic development continue to flourish in a sea of underdevelopment.[12] Not surprisingly, in this view, the gap between rich and poor nations, and between the rich and the poor within nations, grows larger. In this view, underdevelopment is simply the other side of the coin of development; the capitalist world economy produces both.

These patterns are clear in countries like the U.S. too, and in the 1960s, activists, especially blacks and women, began to question prevailing views. As they looked more closely at their own experience and at the data, they began to see a much different reality from that promoted by the prophets of post-industrial society. Thirty per cent of American families remain poor by official government standards, unable to secure the basic necessities of life. Another 20 to 30 per cent are getting by, but unable to save for emergencies, or their children's education. Less than 20 per cent of all American families are able to afford the affluent lifestyles which so dominate the media.[13] Specifically in terms of work, critical examination of the data reveals that the actual size of the working class has not declined significantly since World War II and is not likely to in the foreseeable future; about 60 per cent of American workers work at jobs that involve essentially rote, manual labour.[14] Moreover, there is clear evidence that continuing refinements of managerial techniques and of technology, toward the goal of better control of workers, are transforming many traditional middle-class jobs into working-class jobs.[15]

It is clear that even within advanced capitalist countries like the U.S. different groups of people are channelled into the economy in unequal ways, in different places and times. This is especially clear in the case of Blacks. For they have been channelled into the least desirable, poorest paying jobs; this division of labour can best be explained against the background of the world economy which has involved a racist division of labour since its origins,[16] and in terms of the structure of the internal labour market in the U.S. which has been shaped by the use of racist ideology in management efforts to control the workforce and by reliance on black workers as a reserve army of the unemployed.[17] Women, too, have been channelled into the least desirable, poorest paying jobs; this sexist division of labour can best be explained in terms of the sexist division of labour and emotion inherited from earlier modes of social organisation but transformed and often intensified under capitalism, evident both in the 'private' sphere centred around the family, and thus at the very centre of the psychodynamics of socialisation and personal development, and in the labour market in the historical reliance on women as a reserve army of the unemployed.[18]

In sum, the U.S. and other First World nations may well offer to other capitalist nations an image of their own future development. For, through the growth of transnational corporations, based in the First World, management and production technologies are being diffused throughout the world. On the basis of the U.S. experience, however, this kind of 'development' can only mean an intensification of class, racial and sexual divisions.[19]

The developmentalist perspective may be understood in terms of the experiences in the post-war era in the U.S. of upwardly-mobile, professional, technical, and managerial middle-class workers who celebrated their experience and universalised it into a salvation history for all. But this salvation history has not been adequate to the experience of a majority of the people in the world, or even to a majority in the U.S. Moreover, in the name of science, these theories obscured the exploitative nature of the system, and the courage and strength of ordinary people in the struggles to humanise it in whatever incomplete and distorted forms this has occurred. The result has been that people too often blame themselves for failures to make it in a system where the odds are so high against them, a fact that helps to explain the various forms of pathology that accompany unemployment, mentioned at the beginning of this essay. A new interpretation of work and its meaning in our lives is needed.

3. THEOLOGICAL AGENDA

The theologies of work and leisure referred to above run the risk of being mere ideological justifications for the *status quo*, because they have failed to address the issue of the actual structures of work and division of labour; they seem to presume that the ideals of work and leisure they project already exist.

The analysis sketched here in the context of the world system perspective, however, reveals that the meaning of work cannot be interpreted apart from the larger division of labour in which particular jobs are embedded. This means that the fundamental issue concerns the nature of capitalism as a mode of production, and of its historic alternative, socialism. Ultimately this is a question of nothing less than a new world order.[20]

Recently, Christians around the world have begun to define this issue as a fundamental theological issue.[21] As it concerns the meaning of work it must be looked at from two directions. In a world where the basic needs of the majority of people are unmet, even work that is otherwise alienating can take on a certain dignity when it is oriented toward meeting these needs. But the possibility of reorienting national economies and ultimately the world economy to meet these needs depends on ordinary people, many of whom work at alienating jobs. In this light, the problem with the capitalist division of labour is not only that it is oriented to private profit and not to human needs, and thus excludes all those who do not contribute to higher profits, but that in so fragmenting workers within the system it tends to distort our abilities to see these problems and to do anything about them.[22] As one worker said, herself a white collar worker in the professional sector: 'Most of us have jobs that are too small for our spirit.'[23] For these reasons, our salvation is inseparable from the structures of work and our struggles to transform them.

Notes

1. *The Wealth of Nations* (New York 1937) p. 734.

2. Undoubtedly Marx has been the most influential critic of capitalism; see his *Economic and Philosophic Manuscripts of 1844, Collected Works* (New York 1975) 3 pp. 229-346; and *Capital* (New York 1906) 1 ch. 2.

3. M. Kohn *Class and Conformity* (Chicago 1977) p. 164.

4. Kohn *ibid.*

5. Kohn *op. cit.* p. 189.

6. Communist nations like those in Russia and China are claimed to be pathological deviations from the normal path of development, 'diseases of transition' from traditional to modern society; see W. W. Rostow *The Stages of Economic Growth* (Cambridge 1961).

7. See Lee Cormie 'The Sociology of National Development and Salvation History' in G. Baum ed., *Sociology and Human Destiny* (New York forthcoming).

8. For a critical review of these theologies see F. S. Fiorenza 'Critical Theology and Work' in H. Heisler and J. Houck edd. *A Matter of Dignity* (Notre Dame 1977) pp. 34-37.

9. See, for example, M. D. Chenu *The Theology of Work,* trans L. Soiron (Chicago 1963) (*Pour une theologie du travail* [Paris 1955]).

10. See, for example, K. Rahner 'Theological Remarks on the Problem of Leisure' in *Theological Investigations* trans. K. Smythe (New York 1966) 4 (*Schriften zur Theologie* [Einsiedeln 1961] 4).

11. See S. Amin *Accumulation on a World Scale,* trans. B. Pierce (New York 1974) (L'Accumulation à l'échelle mondiale [Dakar 1970]); I. Wallerstein *The Modern World System* (New York 1974).

12. See the Report of the São Paulo Justice and Peace Commission *São Paulo: Growth and Poverty* (London 1978).

13. See R. Parker *The Myth of the Middle Class* (New York 1972).

14. A. Levinson *The Working Class Majority* (Baltimore 1975).

15. See Special Task Force to the Secretary of Health, Education and Welfare *Work in America* (Cambridge, Mass. 1973) p. 20.

16. See Wallerstein *The Modern World System,* quoted in note 11, at pp. 86 ff.

17. See W. Wilson, *The Declining Significance of Race* (Chicago 1978).

18 See H. B. Saffioti *Women in Class Society,* trans. M. Vale (New York 1978) (*A Mulher na sociedale de classes* [São Paulo 1969]); I. Zaretsky, *Capitalism, the Family and Personal Life* (New York 1976).

19. See The Wellesley Editorial Committee *Women and National Development* (Chicago 1977); see also the special issue of *Southeast Asia Chronicle* No. 66 (Jan.-Feb. 1979) on 'The Changing Role of Southeast Asian Women: The Global Assembly Line and the Social Manipulation of Women on the Job'.

20. In general, no nation can stand as a model for the development of others, since, in addition to differences in cultural, religious, economic, and political traditions and institutions, a nation's location in the world system at the time of development and the shape of the system itself profoundly shape its possibilities for development. In particular, existing socialist societies currently exist within a capitalist world economy and their internal policies must inevitably reflect the

realities of having to deal in the world market on capitalist terms. For this reason, none can stand as the incarnation of the ideal towards which others are striving.

Similarly, the positive effects of efforts at workplace democracy and the limitations of this approach as an effort to transform capitalism must be understood in the context of global economy.

21. J. L. Segundo 'Capitalism versus Socialism: A Theological Crux' (trans. J. P. Donnelly) in C. Geffré and G. Gutierres edd. *The Mystical and Political Dimension of the Christian Faith* (Concilium 96) (New York 1974) 105-123; S. Torres and V. Fabella edd. *The Emergent Gospel* (Maryknoll 1978); A. Boesak *A Farewell to Innocence* (Maryknoll 1977); C. Desmond *Christians or Capitalists?* (London 1977).

22. Contrary to Kohn's hypothesis, this is more a problem for middle-class workers than for others; see M. Maccoby *The Gamesman* (New York 1978).

23. Quoted in S. Terkel *Working* (New York 1975) p. 29.

Contributors

SILVANO BURGALASSI was born in Bibbona in the province of Livorno in 1921. He was ordained after attending the seminary of Pisa, took a degree in social sciences at the Catholic University of Milan, and was a parish priest till 1976. He has lectured in sociology and religious sociology at various universities, and now teaches at both the University of Pisa and the Catholic University of Milan. He is a member of the editorial committee of the Religious Sociology section of *Concilium* and has so far published some 190 books and articles on sociological and pastoral questions.

LEE CORMIE was born in 1943 in Troy, New York (U.S.A.). He has taught in the areas of theology and the social sciences at St Francis Seminary, School of Pastoral Ministry, and is currently teaching in The Divinity School, University of Chicago. He is also Executive Secretary of the Theologians Project of Theology in the Americas; this is a five-year ecumenical project bringing together social activists, church leaders, theologians, and social scientists with the aim of contributing to the revitalisation of theology and theological education through commitment to justice and liberation for the oppressed. He is currently engaged in research and writing on the political economic history of the United States and its role in the world economy, on Black, feminist, and Latin American liberation theologies, and on theological method.

FRANCIS SCHÜSSLER FIORENZA is associate professor at the Catholic University of America. The subject of his doctoral thesis in the University of Münster was *Eschatology and Progress,* a study of Ernst Bloch's philosophy of history. He has published a critical edition of Schleiermacher's *Sendschreiben an Dr Lücke.* He has published articles in *Mysterium Salutis Horizons, Heythrop Journal, Theology Digest,*

Interpretation, Review of Religious Studies, Philosophical Forum, and *Philosophy Today*. He is married to Elisabeth Schüssler Fiorenza, a New Testament Scholar at Notre Dame University and a member of the *Concilium* Editorial Board.

JULIEN FREUND was born in 1921 at Henridorff in Lorraine. He has a degree in philosophy and was a schoolteacher until 1940. During the war he was a member of the French resistance, was imprisoned in several camps and prisons and escaped to live in the 'maquis' until the liberation. He founded the journal *L'Avenir Lorrain* and for a time did research in his subject in the Centre National de la Recherche Scientifique. He has been professor of sociology at Strasbourg University since 1965, founding the Institut de Polémologie and the Centre for study and research into the social sciences there. He was the first to translate the work of Max Weber into French and his own published works include: *L'Essence du politique* (Paris 1965); *La Sociologie de Max Weber* (Paris 1966); *Le Nouvel age* (Paris 1970); *Théories des sciences humaines* (Paris 1973); *Pareto* (Paris 1974) and *Utopie et viole* (Paris 1978). Most of these books have been translated into several languages. He has also written numerous articles which have been published in French and many other languages.

FRANCOIS HOUTART was born in Belgium in 1925. He gained a doctorate in sociology in the Catholic University of Louvain (1973). He has been Director of the Centre of Socio-religious research since 1956 and is professor at the Catholic University of Louvain. He has written many works on the Sociology of Religion, including: *Eglisex et révolution* (with A. Rousseau, 1971) and *Religion and Ideology in Sri Lanka* (Hansa 1974).

GENEVIÈVE LEMERCINIER was born in Belgium in 1923, and gained a doctorate in sociology at the University of Louvain in 1977. She is an Associate of the Centre for socio-religious research at the Catholic University of Louvain.

OTTO MADURO was born in Caracas (Venezuela) in 1945. He holds a doctorate in the philosophy of religion and a degree in the sociology of religion, and has been associate professor in the University of the Andes in Mérida (Venezuela) since 1969. He has written a number of books and articles on marxism and religion, including, *Marxismo y religion* (1977).

WŁADYSŁAW PIWOWARSKI was born in Poland in 1929. After philosophical and theological studies, he studied social science at the

Catholic University of Lublin. He gained his doctorate in social science at Lublin in 1961 and has lectured there from 1961 to 1967, at the same time doing research into religion in Poland, and became professor of the sociology of religion in 1970. In 1976/77 he was senior research fellow at the Yale Divinity School. Professor Piwowarski has published widely on the sociology of religion, the sociology of morality, social philosophy and Catholic social teaching.

JEAN RÉMY was born in Soumange (Belgium) in 1928. He graduated in philosophy and obtained his doctorate in economics at the University of Louvain, at which he is now a professor in the Faculty of Political and Social Sciences and Director of the Centres for Socio-Religious Research and Urban and Rural Sociology. His publications include *La Ville, phénomène économique* (Brussels 1968); (with F. Boulard) 'Catholicisme urbain et pratique religieuse—Villes et régions culturelles. Acquis et débats' (*Archives de Sociologie des Religions* no. 29, 1970); (with F. Houtart) three volumes on the Church and contemporary civilisation: I. *Milieu urbain et communauté chrétienne,* II. *Eglise et société en mutation,* III. *Sacerdoce, autorité et innovation dans l'Eglise* (1968-70); with L. Voyé *La Ville et l'urbanisation* (1974).

FRANCISCO ROLIM has a doctorate in sociology from the State University of São Paulo and is assistant professor of Fluminense Federal University.

RUDOLF SIEBERT was born in Frankfurt a.M. (Germany) in 1927. He studied history, theology, philosophy and philology at the Universities of Mainz and Munster, Germany, and at the Catholic University of America, Washington, D.C., U.S.A. He first taught in Germany and then in the U.S.A. and Canada. Since 1965 he has been professor of religion and society in the Religion Department of Western Michigan University, Kalamazoo, Michigan, U.S.A., teaching courses on the psychology, sociology, philosophy and theology of religion. He is also the founder of the Center of Humanistic Future Studies at Western Michigan University, and he has initiated and is directing the international course on *The Future of Religion* in the Inter-University Centre for Post-Graduate Studies in Dubrovnik, Yugoslavia. He was written widely on the critical theory and political theology. Recent books include the following: *Hegel's Philosophy of History; Theological, Humanistic and Scientific Elements* (Washington, D.C. 1979); *Horkheimer's Critical Sociology of Religion: The Relative and the Transcendent* (Washington, D.C. 1979); *Critical Theory of Religion* (New York 1980).

JOHN SIMPSON was educated at Seattle Pacific University, Princeton Theological Seminary, and Stanford University. He is Associate Professor of Sociology and Associate Director, Centre for Religious Studies, University of Toronto. The topic of his current research is high gods in primitive societies.

SRDJAN VRCAN was born in 1922 in Split (Yugoslavia), and gained a doctorate in Philosophy of the University of Zagreb. He is now professor of sociology at the Law School of the University of Split and co-director of the Seminar on the Future of Religion at the Inter-University Centre for Post-Graduate Studies in Dubrovnik. His publications include: *Problemi radničkog samoupravljanja u nekim industrijskim radnim organizacijama u Dalmaciji* (Some Problems of the Workers Self-Management in some Industrial Organisations in Dalmatia) (Split 1968); *Drustvene nejednakosti i moderno drudtvo* (Social Inequalities and Modern Society) (Zagreb 1974); 'Religion and Irreligion in a Socialist Society' in *Social Compass* 19 (1972) 2; 'Some Theoretical Implications of the Religiosity as a Mass Phenomenon in a Socialist Society' in *C.I.S.R. Acts* (Lille 1971); 'Working-class Commitment to Religion and Church' in *C.I.S.R. Acts* (Lille 1977); 'Sociologija religije kao "ancilla theologiae"?' ('Sociology of Religion as "Ancilla Theologiae"?') in *Sociologija* 20 (1978) 2-3.

CLAUS WESTERMANN was born in 1909. He was pastor in Berlin for a number of years but since 1949 he has been teaching in university. He was professor at the Kirchliche Hochschule, Berlin, and since 1958 he has been professor of Old Testament Studies at the University of Heidelberg. His publications include: *Das Loben Gottes in den Psalmen* (1953; 5th ed. 1977 under the title *Lob und Klage in den Psalmen*); *Forschung am Alten Testament* (1964) I, (1974) II (with complete bibliography); *Biblischer Kommentar zum Alten Testament, Neukirchen,* I,1*Genesis* (1974).

CONCILIUM

Religion in the Eighties

A multi-volume library of contemporary religious thought • published in 10 volumes annually • exploring the latest trends and developments in the Sociology of Religion, Liturgy, Dogma, Practical Theology, Fundamental Theology, Canon Law, Ecumenism, Spirituality and Moral Theology

CONTRIBUTORS

JEAN RÉMY · OTTO MADURO · JULIEN FREUND
FRANÇOIS HOUTART AND GENEVIÈVE LEMERCINIER
FRANCISCO ROLIM · JOHN SIMPSON
WLADYSLAW PIWORWARSKY · SRDJAN VRCAN
CLAUS WESTERMANN · FRANCIS SCHUESSLER FIORENZA
SILVANO BURGALASSI · RUDOLF SIEBERT
LEE CORMIE

THE SEABURY PRESS, NEW YORK T. &. T. CLARK, EDINBURGH